THE ART OF CREATING WEALTH
A Millennial, Gen Z, and Gen X Guide to Navigating Life's Struggles

eBook: 979-8-9985198-1-9
Paperback: 979-8-9985198-2-6

Cover design by Sooraj Mathew

Edited by Hilary Jastram

┌ **Bookmark** ┐
└──── PUBLISHING HOUSE ────┘

THE ART OF
CREATING
WEALTH

MARIO V. SICARI

A MILLENNIAL, GEN Z, AND GEN X GUIDE TO NAVIGATING LIFE'S STRUGGLES

DEDICATION

This book is dedicated to the countless people I have helped to create wealth over the years.

It is also dedicated to my family, who have supported me unconditionally.

Finally, it is dedicated to my staff, who, through their commitment, will carry on my legacy.

GET IN TOUCH

✉ Mario.sicari@bgs-fg.com

TABLE OF CONTENTS

INTRODUCTION

Welcome to the world of investing, a realm where the prudent and the adventurous alike seek to navigate the ever-changing movements of financial markets in pursuit of prosperity.

In this book, you'll journey through the fundamentals, strategies, and philosophies that underpin successful investing. You'll also explore the impacts of geopolitics, social and mainstream media on society, a failed educational system that affects people just like you, and a positive framework designed to empower you.

My experiences have led to my success today, which includes a nationally recognized business ranking as one of the nation's top independent wealth advisory firms. If there is anything I can take away from my years on this planet, it is that life is uncharted. Where you are today is likely not where you will be in years to come—and that is okay. Life is filled with opportunities every day.

Allow me to share my knowledge to inspire you to seize opportunities, leaving no stones unturned. Whether creating wealth, empowering yourself, or discovering your strengths to achieve success, it is up to you to make the call. This book will guide you through the obstacles you will face and, better, give you the tools you need to help avoid them as much as possible. I will teach you about investing, patience, and, most importantly, how to succeed.

Before we begin, you need to accept that investing is both an art and a science; it blends analytical rigor with intuitive insight. It demands patience, discipline, and the willingness to embrace uncertainty.

The beautiful part is that within this uncertainty lies opportunity—the chance for you to grow wealth, achieve financial independence, and realize your dreams. Yes, it's possible for all people—the difference is taking the time to learn the right aspects of what you are about to do. It's about not being rash and jumping right in. I will explain more about that in a minute.

As the world of finance evolves and technologies advance, the investing landscape continues to transform. The distractions of today's world add another dimension and the unintended consequences of taking you away from your goals. We are all fighting to stay centered on what matters most despite the geopolitical landscape, social media in our faces all the time, 24-hour news, legacy media, and talk radio programming—which is disguised as accurate reporting of current events and news. Modern-day schools, universities, and colleges have now taken on the role of forming opinions and stirring controversy. There have never been as many distractions as there are today.

Did you know these topics are as much about investing as any other? They are because, as you are about to discover, a huge part of investing is staying the course. So, I will attempt to rationalize much of the "noise" and clarify the rhetoric to help you form your own opinions.

I wrote this book to equip you with the tools and, most importantly, the mindset needed to thrive in the investing world—whether you are a seasoned stock picker or just starting your journey. From understanding the principles of risk and return to exploring the intricacies of asset allocation and portfolio management, you will find what you need within these pages to get started creating lasting wealth.

Investing encompasses more than knowing the numbers on a screen or charts in a report. It's about aligning your potential purchases with your values, goals, and aspirations. It's about building a better future for yourself, your loved ones, and the world around you.

As you delve into the pages ahead, you will be encouraged to seek financial success and consider the broader impact of your investments on society. I wrote this book through the lens of what has worked for me in refusing many of life's distractions, only proving my point that life's journey is a struggle. But with proper guidance, the journey can be rewarding. This book will prepare you for staying focused. Yes, some setbacks are inevitable, but many can be avoided if you are just made aware of what they are and know there are some helpful options for getting past them.

MY BACKGROUND

At an early age, I struggled with my identity. I grew up in a strict family in a very comfortable home, but I had a hard time in school. I think this had more to do with me not applying myself than any type of learning disability. I spoke Italian at home and English outside. I was a hustler at a young age, pushing my lawn mower around the neighborhood and cutting lawns for cash. I would rake leaves in the fall and shovel snow-covered driveways in the winter.

In high school, I wanted to do nothing else but play basketball. As my parents were immigrants, they saw no value in it. My dad owned a bakery and insisted I work after school and on weekends. I was disappointed then, but as I got older, I appreciated that those experiences molded me into the individual I am today.

Growing up, I had many different jobs, from bartending to disc jockeying in a famous New York City nightclub. I also went to school and studied electrical engineering. I was very motivated.

3

Then, my brother wanted me to partner with him in a grocery store, so I quit my job as an electrical contractor and walked away from a career. We owned a successful business for 12 years. Around that time, I discovered something was missing from my life. Despite being married with three great kids and all my life experiences, I felt unaccomplished. So, I sought the help of a life coach, Dr. Henry Benvenisti. He helped identify who I was, but more importantly, who I could be. He helped me recognize and harness the effectiveness of understanding the five most important personality traits: extraversion, agreeableness, openness, conscientiousness, and neuroticism. Extraversion is sociability, agreeableness is kindness, openness is creativity and intrigue, conscientiousness is thoughtfulness, and neuroticism often involves sadness or emotional instability. Being able to identify these traits is paramount to building character.

Then, I picked up the first book I had read in a long time, titled *I'm OK—You're OK*, and I transformed myself into the person I needed to be. More importantly, I was able to sustain the vision.

The next most pivotal step in my life happened by accident. My close friend, Tom, asked if he could come to my home to talk to me about what he was doing. Little did I know, he wanted to sell me an investment fund. When he found out I had begun investing at 24 and wasn't interested in what he was selling, I gave him a presentation about my investment experience. His only recourse to salvage the appointment was recruiting me to work in his family-owned business. He didn't have to ask me twice. This was just what I was looking for—an opportunity.

Within two months, I had my securities license. I enrolled in an online college and began studying for my degree in finance. Within three years, after a tremendous amount of sacrifice, hard work, and dedication while working two jobs, I decided it was time to walk out from the family business and became a regional sales manager for CJM Planning Corp. Shortly after, I was promoted to VP of business development and held a senior executive position within the firm. I had completed my studies with more letters at the end of my name than *in* my name. I was 40 years old.

My path has led me to this place and compelled me to share my experiences so that you will believe nothing is unachievable if you just focus on what matters and avoid distractions.

> *Please know that before you can understand investing,*
> *certain aspects of your life must be met with an open mind.*

Ultimately, investing is a journey of discovery, growth, and empowerment. It's about taking control of your financial destiny and shaping your desired future. As you explore the principles, strategies, and wisdom that define the art and science of investing, you will find that embarking on it can be enriching.

The current financial markets are characterized by a blend of optimism and uncertainty and are shaped by myriad factors, including economic indicators, geopolitical tensions, technological advancements, and societal shifts. Despite our unprecedented access to information, resources, and investment opportunities today, many struggle to accumulate long-term wealth, most notably because of the behavioral aspect of investing—which directly influences our reaction to these indicators, tensions, advancements, and shifts.

Not to mention, the very makeup of our human psychology often leads to emotional decision-making, such as succumbing to fear during market downturns or greed during periods of euphoria. These emotions can drive investors to make impulsive decisions that deviate from their long-term investment plans, which can hinder wealth accumulation.

After reading this book, it is my greatest intention that you will not be one of those impulsive or fearful investors.

Spoiler alert: sometimes, the best action is to do nothing, even while everyone else is in panic mode and irrational behavior takes over.

One fact is certain: market sell-offs are common and can last days, weeks, and months. I will train you to stay focused on your long-term strategies and constantly remind you that this is a marathon, not a sprint to the finish line. Removing the emotional factor is difficult; you must learn to trust yourself and believe in your journey.

Moreover, the allure of quick profits and speculative trading can tempt people into high-risk strategies that may yield short-term gains but often lead to significant losses over time. Market timing, chasing trends, and attempting to outsmart the market are risky endeavors that frequently result in underperformance compared to a disciplined, long-term investment approach. These temptations can be mitigated with information. When you know that fearful movements will likely not yield what you are seeking, you will be prepared to stand firm and stick to your long-term plan. Truthfully, very few stable and wealthy individuals get that way by making impulsive choices.

Additionally, a lack of financial literacy and education can contribute to suboptimal investment decisions. Many people enter the financial markets without a clear understanding of basic investment principles, asset allocation strategies, or risk management techniques. You must educate yourself before you take a first step or any step. Don't feel rushed to bypass the knowledge of others who have come before you and who might've learned the hard way. Everyone starts from the same place of curiosity. Those who go on to become successful have given themselves the grace to learn.

Without a solid foundation of knowledge, you can fall prey to misinformation, investment scams, or overly complex products that do not align with your financial goals.

Furthermore, structural barriers such as high fees, limited access to investment opportunities, and systemic inequalities like lack of education and financial resources can impede wealth accumulation, particularly for marginalized communities. Typically, those who do not have enough money or the right social connections will invest too little or not at all. Without equitable access to resources and opportunities, you might face an uphill battle toward building sustainable long-term wealth. That's the last thing I want for you. And I know you don't want that, either, or you wouldn't have picked up this book.

As we discuss these topics in relation to the state of our country and investing, my goal is not to change your views, political affiliation, or conclusions about current events but to offer a rational understanding of how a never-ending source of information constantly manipulates us.

One friend and client spent countless hours watching 24-hour cable news and listening to countless hours of talk radio. His opinions were not his own, and he constantly repeated what he heard on the radio.

After listening to him talk about something insignificant to both of us, I asked him, "Why?" As in, "Why are you sharing this with me?" He couldn't answer me.

I asked him, "Can you elaborate about *your* feelings on the issue?" He couldn't.

I then explained, "The reason you can't give me a rational answer is because you are being manipulated and programmed to form irrational opinions and parrot the narrative."

The good news is that his investments continued to grow under my watch, and he finally realized he had wasted years on the time and "noise" of listening to these distractions that could have hurt his potential to earn money and think for himself.

After his wife of 20 years passed, he decided to focus on himself and what was most important to him, his quality of life, and his daughter. Today, he is retired and enjoys fishing and spending time with her.

STAY OPEN

I invite you to begin reading about the coming topics with an open mind. As you do so, please remember the most important ingredient in creating wealth: TIME. No other factors can affect your investments as much, so please proceed with caution and understand that when something sounds too good to be true, it probably is. Get-rich schemes never work out. Don't be afraid of risk, but know that with it comes rewards.

The next few chapters are geared toward self-improvement. You might ask yourself, *what is the purpose of reading about this topic in a book designed to help me create wealth?* The answer is that dealing with life's struggles is a distraction that will derail your journey. Be patient and continue reading.

"If you could kick the person in the pants responsible for your troubles, you wouldn't sit for a month."
—Theodore Roosevelt

CHAPTER 1

Building My
Distraction-Free Legacy

To continue my story with the assurance that I am a credible wealth and legacy-building source, you must know I began putting my money to work at a young age and that I stayed the course, rejecting distraction.

I began investing at the age of 24 when I opened my first mutual fund account, American Century Growth Fund. At the time, I worked nights as a bartender and days as an industrial mechanic. On weekends, I somehow found myself working part-time in a friend's bagel shop.

With full-time and part-time salaries and all my time accounted for, I couldn't spend money on fancy cars or exotic trips. Bartending money went directly into my mutual fund account monthly. This lack of time was awesome because, at times, I could save $700 per week.

When my brother approached me with the idea of going into business, my father decided to assist us by becoming a partner. After 15 years of 7-day workweeks and long days with no quality of life, I felt helpless and trapped, my self-esteem nonexistent, so I sought the advice of a therapist, who helped me identify my self-worth. He motivated me with the small task of setting goals. That's when I turned a corner in my life, never to go back. I began the process of empowering myself to believe there was nothing I could not accomplish.

Empowering myself required setting achievable expectations and understanding that time was on my side.

After years of despair, I focused on improving my quality of life by setting goals and running to manage stress and mental tension. Running can be a time for reflection, problem-solving, and generating fresh perspectives. You may want to consider building this habit yourself.

At 35, I returned to school and worked toward my degree in finance, all while grinding away in the family business and supporting a family of five. I cannot begin to describe the sacrifice I made (or my level of exhaustion).

Shortly after I enrolled in school, I met my mentor, a kind, generous, and supportive man who believed in my abilities. Years earlier, he had founded a small family-owned broker-dealer where he worked with his sons. He gave me the opportunity to secure my securities licenses with his firm. After a few short years, the firm offered me an opportunity to become part of the management team. I made a life-changing decision to leave the family business and work in the financial services field full-time. My decision, at first, seemed selfish to some and created family resentment, but with time, feelings healed.

This period in my life taught me that family is precious and that business and family don't always mix. My father always envisioned building his legacy and passing it on to his children. But I watched him as I grew up and as I set out to do my own thing. That's how I learned that one man's dream can never be another man's reality. For years, as I was growing up, family time didn't occur to my father—his only goal was to build a family business. Although his intentions were well-intentioned, they were misplaced and created resentment. At least I applied those lessons to my life.

Choosing a different profession in a totally different field was a difficult decision, but it was for the best. Had it not been for my therapist's help in identifying my abilities in the financial industry, I don't know where I would be today. Talking to him was life-changing.

After three years of working in the financial services industry, I became vice president of business development. My experience, networking, and commitment to my career led to my recognition among industry leaders as a pioneer and visionary in the asset management space.

The firm was soon acquired through an acquisition, and I was again placed in a position to make a choice; the risk was again significant. Many firms needed my expertise. I was aware of the mergers and acquisitions occurring in the broker-dealer space and did not want to settle for another short-lived opportunity.

A third-party asset management partner I had leveraged to build the asset management division I had previously worked for was interested in hiring me. I met with the two brothers who founded the firm. After a four-hour meeting, the CEO told me he would take me on if I wanted the position. Then, in the next breath, he offered me another opportunity, saying, "You have all the necessary knowledge and tools to build your own successful firm. I suggest you do so."

Thankfully, over the years I had developed the skill to reach inside and motivate myself to create something remarkable. I had done so much internal work that I was comfortable having ultimate control over my future—with no one else managing me. With no capital to speak of and a few great colleagues, I started BGS Capital Management in 2004; today, we are a successful wealth management firm with over $300 million under management as of January 1st, 2025. I have utilized my years of experience to manage, mentor, and motivate a new generation of advisors.

Over the years, BGS Capital Management has been recognized as a leader in customer service and satisfaction. Today, our staff consists of seven dedicated individuals who have committed themselves to carrying on a legacy and who work countless hours each week helping clients reach their dreams. That's a pretty motivating mission.

Building a firm out of thin air took hard work, dedication, time, commitment, and sacrifice. Today, financial independence has led me to a comfortable quality of life.

I share my story with you in the hope that it will inspire you to believe that nothing is unachievable. Everything is possible.

We're not that much different in terms of getting started. One of the greatest tactics I ever deployed for myself was the ability to stay focused. If you can do this, you will be more productive than the majority of the world.

In addition to my career in financial services, I volunteer my time to my community and have served on its board of education for seven years. I have also served on numerous township boards and worked locally with both political parties. Many of my experiences have formed my views of the current system. As I have stated, my goal is not to change your views or perceptions but to share my perspective and urge you to think in-depth about the decisions you want to make that resonate with your values.

I hope I can also influence you to recognize the "noise" and constant gaslighting and propaganda used to create fear and form society's views. It's unfair to be subjected to it and feel as though we must fight it off, but the more you condition yourself to do so, the more you will be able to think freely and without bias. In most circumstances, fear-mongering is intended to ensure power to a specific political party or belief system. Now that you know that it's time to get busy examining what you do want to adhere to, learning tactics to strengthen your self-empowerment, and resisting distractions to build your empire.

*"One must learn to think well before learning to think;
afterward, it proves too difficult."*
—Anatole France

CHAPTER 2

Empowerment

Self-empowerment is the process of an individual taking deliberate actions to enhance their sense of control, confidence, and agency. It involves recognizing and leveraging one's strengths, abilities, and resources to pursue personal goals, overcome challenges, and navigate life's complexities.

Understanding your strengths, weaknesses, values, and goals is fundamental to your self-empowerment. Reaching a level where you believe you can make decisions and successfully navigate problems in all areas of your life involves introspection, reflection, and a willingness to confront the positive and negative aspects of whatever you are dealing with. That quality is known as self-awareness.

Believing in your abilities and potential is essential for empowerment. Developing a positive mindset, cultivating self-confidence, and challenging self-limiting beliefs are central to building your rock-solid self-belief that you will accomplish specific tasks or goals. When you set achievable goals, take incremental steps, and experience success, you can enhance your sense of self-efficacy and empowerment.

Self-empowered people take responsibility for their choices and actions rather than relying solely on external factors or influences. They assert autonomy and actively shape their paths in life. Do you see yourself here? Is this an area where you would like to improve? It's okay if you answered yes. You're being honest about the new trajectory you want for yourself—and that is the first step to improving anything.

Embracing a growth mindset and a commitment to lifelong learning are essential for self-empowerment. This means not assuming that you have all the answers, which is a very tough lesson for us all to learn, but it is critical to moving yourself beyond where you are now. You can get there by seeking out new experiences, acquiring new skills, and adapting to changing circumstances.

You will constantly be challenged by changing circumstances and failures. Developing resilience is the ability to bounce back from setbacks, challenges, and failures. When you are self-empowered, you cultivate resilience by viewing obstacles as opportunities for growth, learning from adversity, and persisting in the face of setbacks. In fact, the most frustrating challenges, which can drive us crazy can also drive the greatest growth.

> *Everyone wants the knowledge; no one wants to gain it through trials and pain.*

Self-empowerment is a dynamic and ongoing process that involves personal growth, self-discovery, and the cultivation of inner strength and resilience. I am pushing you to learn to take ownership of your life while you are younger and to actively pursue your goals to enhance your well-being, fulfillment, and overall quality of life. Is it going to be easy? Of course not. So, prepare yourself however you must, but know that a life lived with discipline is much easier to endure and prepares you for the unexpected, giving you a greater shot at getting through challenges in better shape.

Understanding and embracing the tenets of your individuality is paramount for setting goals. Placing your needs first and foremost, often referred to as self-care or self-prioritization, means maintaining overall well-being and achieving a balanced life. It's a daily practice involving recognizing your needs, setting boundaries, and taking deliberate actions to meet those needs. By placing your well-being first, you not only improve your quality of life you also enhance your ability to support and engage with others effectively. In short, you will know and practice the healthiest ways to take care of yourself, and so you will treat others the same way. Strive to find a sustainable balance, as it will allow you to thrive in all areas of your life.

There are so many examples of individuals who take risks to succeed in life through self-motivation and a simple dream. Take, for example, the reality show *Shark Tank,* where entrepreneurs pitch their business ideas to a panel of successful investors, known as "sharks," in hopes of securing investment funding. The show provides a platform for self-starters and inventors to showcase their products or services and for the sharks to negotiate and potentially invest in promising ventures.

Before I go any further, let me say that I am in no way advising a strategy to appear on the show. I mention the show because some contestants are extremely self-motivated and have empowered themselves with a vision of success. There is a fire in their eyes that they will sacrifice and work hard, yet they often fail. But their failures are not something to lament. They are inspiring because these go-getters refuse to give up. When they fall, they get back up and continue to work hard.

It is impossible to empower yourself with distractions, and these contenders know this. They would not be standing on the stage if they had permitted their attention to be drawn to the endless distractions that tempt us all.

Except for loved ones, people, in general, are not interested in your personal goals and aspirations, and while your goals (yes, even business goals) should be personal, measurable, and attainable, your mind and thoughts must be clear of distractions if you want to hit your targets. Many distractions can cause us to lose focus. We might be tempted to read about drama perpetuated by misinformation and exaggerations spread by so-called mainstream media news outlets, political rhetoric from elected officials and candidates, and professors and teachers who, at times, use their position and credibility as educators to promote their own values.

"You've gotta keep control of your time, and you can't unless you say no.
You can't let people set your agenda in life."
—Warren Buffett

I will speak to you constantly about "distractions" and "noise" regardless of the main topic. Society has built a reputation of different members of the "grievance" crowd standing on soap boxes, screaming loudly, and demanding attention—all intended to manipulate and gain access to an audience. This is where I want you to be careful and not allow yourself to fall into a trap. Being informed about current events is smart, but knowing the facts and understanding and acknowledging the source is critical.

Many media outlets, pundits, legislators, and members of academia reside in an echo chamber. They have built careers and amassed fortunes by manipulating the masses. The echo chamber is an analogy describing how beliefs are amplified or reinforced by communication and repetition inside a closed system. You can understand the inherent dangers of such an environment, which, among other implications, can significantly limit exposure to different or competing viewpoints.

The echo chamber phenomenon is common in various contexts across social media, news consumption, and social interactions. Within an echo chamber, members predominantly share the same opinions, beliefs, and biases. Divergent perspectives are rare or if they do arise, are actively suppressed. Information and beliefs are continuously repeated, reinforcing members' existing views and making them more resistant to change—the basis for the echo anthology.

> *Members of an echo chamber tend to seek out information sources that confirm their preexisting beliefs and avoid those that challenge them—also called virtue signaling.*

Opposing viewpoints are often dismissed, ridiculed, or ignored, causing further isolation from any information that might contradict the consensus views. The echo chamber effect is intended to manipulate especially young, impressionable people who have yet to realize their own beliefs and views. Make sure before you turn on the "people pleasing" aspect of your personality to not ruffle feathers that you give yourself every advantage to develop your own opinions and beliefs. Do not fall prey to the perpetrators of these echoes and jump ship to subscribe to an affiliation you may not fully understand—a primary reason such chambers exist. You are stronger than that and deserve the time and ability to figure out what you stand for. You deserve the right to practice self-empowerment and grow it through smart, critical choices.

The consequences of the echo chamber can lead to increased political and social polarization as people become more entrenched in their views and less willing to compromise or understand opposing perspectives. Inaccurate information and false beliefs can also spread rapidly within an echo chamber, as there is little critical scrutiny or fact-checking.

As I mentioned, exposure to only one side of an argument can limit critical thinking skills and the ability to engage with complex issues in a nuanced way. I bring this up again to get you to think about it differently in various avenues, such as when you see it in political candidates pounding the podium for their election or re-election. Be aware.

The only way to keep expanding your mind and mitigate the echo chamber effects is to actively seek out various and diverse news sources and viewpoints that can help break the reinforcement cycle as you adopt critical thinking and skepticism toward all information— even that which aligns with your beliefs. Greater transparency and control over social media algorithms can help you understand and manage the biases in your content feeds. Engaging in conversations with people holding different viewpoints can foster understanding and reduce polarization. It can even bring people and communities together.

Although we have our differences, it is those differences that make us unique.

> *Accept yourself as the person you can be regardless of your religious, political, or personal beliefs. Be the example of empowerment, and never let another's influence manipulate you.*

Work hard, sacrifice, and never fear failure. Believe in yourself and know that you hold the keys to your success. Everyone must experience failure at some point in their lifetime. Failure should be regarded as a teaching mechanism. The experiences of failure and how we adjust to avoid reliving our same failures lead to success.

Setbacks or failures can have a negative impact on how we move forward. I remember when I decided to take up running. I was not in any kind of shape to run long distances. If I attempted to run one mile at a slow pace, the success I wanted to see would have been achievable. I knew I could reach greater distances over time and that my training would also allow my time to improve. These were acceptable terms for a positive outcome, but keep in mind that some days, positive outcomes require more commitment and time. My point is not to give up.

Remember, making life-changing adjustments requires discipline. The first step is to realize that you are not a victim. Never view yourself as a victim. Victimhood culture allows blame-shifting, excuse-making, and self-pity to keep people from being accountable for their actions. Victimhood culture also generates a society of people who identify foremost as being oppressed. You are none of the aforementioned unless you choose to be.

As you turn the page, hold tight to the fact that empowerment will prepare you for a successful life and provide the tools to fulfill dreams and aspirations.

"Take responsibility in your own life, and keep moving forward."
—Mario Sicari

CHAPTER 3

Communication Skills – A Lost Practice

The deterioration of communication skills today is derived from technological advancements, changes in social behavior, and educational priorities. If we are to fix this, it may require a concerted effort to balance digital convenience with the cultivation of traditional communication skills, opening up environments where deep, meaningful, and articulate interactions are encouraged and valued.

The rise of texting, social media, and instant messaging has led to a preference for short, informal communication. Perhaps you can see this reflected in your own life? This adaptation of traditional communication often results in a lack of attention to grammar, spelling, and punctuation, degrading overall writing and verbal skills. The widespread use of emojis, GIFs, and abbreviations (e.g., LOL, BRB) simplifies and shortens how we speak to each other, and it has reduced the need for descriptive language and nuanced expression.

Increased reliance on virtual communication tools like Zoom, Skype, and Teams, especially accelerated by the COVID-19 pandemic, has reduced the frequency of in-person interactions. So, non-verbal cues such as body language, facial expressions, and tone of voice—crucial for effective communication—are often lost or diminished in virtual settings. We also know that many people are spending significant time interacting with digital devices rather than engaging in real-life social interactions, further hindering the development of conversational skills and emotional intelligence.

> *With the rise of video content and social media, people are reading fewer books, articles, and long-form content.*

This reduces exposure to complex vocabulary, varied sentence structures, and well-articulated arguments, so foundational for developing strong communication skills. The habit of skimming through information fostered by the internet rather than deep reading leads to superficial understanding and poor retention, impacting the ability to engage in meaningful discussions.

The constant barrage of information and notifications from smartphones and other devices has shortened attention spans. People are more prone to distraction, making it harder to engage in prolonged, focused conversations. The multi-tasking culture often leads to divided attention, reducing the quality of communication. We all know someone who checks their phone while trying to have a conversation, leading to misunderstandings and a lack of genuine engagement.

While crucial, the emphasis on STEM (science, technology, engineering, mathematics) education has sometimes overshadowed the importance of humanities and social sciences, where communication skills are often honed. Educational systems focused on standardized testing may neglect developing critical thinking and communication skills. Remote learning and test-oriented teaching methods can impede the ability to articulate ideas clearly and persuasively.

Cultural shifts toward casual and informal communication styles can erode the distinction between formal and informal language, impacting professional and academic communication. While promoting diversity, globalization can also dilute language, potentially forcing non-native speakers to rely heavily on simplified language versions. As more dominant languages, such as English, Spanish, and Mandarin, become accepted forms of communication, a loss of minority languages will result and harm grammatical skills within these cultures.

Effective communication is the process of exchanging information, ideas, thoughts, and feelings clearly and concisely. It should be understood by all parties involved. It is crucial in both personal and professional contexts for building relationships, facilitating collaboration, and ensuring tasks are completed efficiently. Messages should be clear and free from ambiguity, which means using simple language and avoiding jargon that may confuse the recipient. Effective communication is often concise. It avoids unnecessary details, making the message easy to understand.

To achieve effective communication, we must also pay attention to what is being said and what we say. Active listening involves fully listening to the speaker, making eye contact, and not interrupting. This shows respect and helps us fully understand the message conveyed. Nodding your head or giving verbal affirmations provides feedback that helps the speaker know their message is being received and comprehended.

Recognizing and appropriately responding to others' emotions can foster better communication. Empathy helps build rapport and trust.

Managing one's emotions, especially in stressful situations, ensures that communication remains effective and does not escalate into conflict.

Nonverbal cues, such as posture, gestures, and facial expressions, can convey a lot of information and should align with the verbal message. The tone and pitch of voice can also influence how the message is received. A calm and steady tone is often more effective than a high-pitched or aggressive one.

Effective communicators are open to new ideas and perspectives, which nurtures a collaborative and inclusive environment. Respecting the viewpoints of others, even when they differ from one's own, is essential for maintaining constructive dialogue.

Asking for feedback ensures that the message has been understood correctly and provides an opportunity for clarification. Repeating or summarizing the other person's words can confirm understanding and prevent miscommunication.

Effective communicators adapt their style to suit the audience and context, whether they are engaging in a formal business meeting or having a casual conversation. When interacting with others, maintain an awareness and respect for cultural differences to prevent misunderstandings and enhance communication. Not every message can be delivered in the same way. Some messages are better received through different channels, such as face-to-face meetings, emails, phone calls, or instant messaging. The choice of medium can affect the clarity and reception of the message.

Effective communication is a skill that involves practicing clear articulation, active listening, empathy, nonverbal cues, respect, feedback, adaptability, and choosing the appropriate communication channels. These elements combined help ensure that messages are conveyed and received accurately, cultivating better understanding and collaboration no matter who you are talking with—your Aunt Sally or your boss at lunch.

The ability to convey ideas clearly and effectively in written form includes using grammar and punctuation and demonstrating the organization of your ideas. Understanding the formalities and conventions of professional email communication, such as appropriate greetings, clarity, and keeping it short, is key if you hope to get your message across effectively. Writing specialized documents such as reports, manuals, and instructions requires the above tools and precision and clarity, which is hard to put into play if you are spending time getting away from these fundamentals.

And look, I'm not saying how you text or instant message people is wrong. But it is distancing you from applying the fundamentals of language that your formal education taught you. The more you practice this shorthand language application, the more it becomes your go-to, meaning the more you will get away from remembering communication basics. I am just urging you not to throw away the old rules entirely. Stay relevant to what you still need to know to get your point across correctly, actively listen, and stay on track professionally—where how you communicate still matters.

It is also important to continually develop human relations. Speak to people and use your verbal skills to communicate. There is nothing as nice as a cheerful word of greeting. Smile at others walking down the street next to you, in line for your latte, or wherever you happen to be; it takes 47 muscles to frown and only 13 to smile. Showing a genuine interest in people, whether you agree or disagree with their philosophical differences, is normal in a diverse world. It is essential to know that communication can develop; it is a living language, and you can find common ground.

As you do your best to engage meaningfully and empathetically with others, be considerate of their feelings. I remind myself that there are usually three sides to a controversy: yours, the other person's, and the right side, backed by facts.

A good sense of humor, a big dose of patience, and a dash of humility will reward you tenfold.

Building relationships is important. Understanding how to keep and maintain them requires moving beyond the communication phase. Communication is the foundation of relationships; it is required to set the stage. When you actively listen, your verbal and non-verbal skills, clarity, and empathy are all working. Your ability to connect with people will set you apart from others. But something else is required to become effective in communication and as a person. That is loyalty.

Loyalty skills can be applied in both personal relationships and business. Interaction between people builds trust. Loyalty connects with a person's core values. Unlike skills, values are intangible but extremely powerful in shaping individuality. Most importantly, loyalty can build strong relationships, social support, and mutual emotional health. Being honest, supportive, respectful, and appreciative fortifies this all-important building block of committed relationships.

Loyalty stands for commitment and dedication to your values and mission statement. It is being true to yourself and is the key to a good night's rest and a clear conscience. Loyalty involves being devoted and vulnerable but never naïve. It is, without question, a risk worth taking.

By making it a habit to practice positive, trust-building behavior, you are likely to achieve lasting loyalty. It is a two-way street. Yes, there is a risk of vulnerability. You will sometimes be let down, but the payoff can be significant. No matter what, you will learn all about it as you navigate life. All you can do as a person is be true to yourself.

"Trust is earned, respect is given, and loyalty is demonstrated. Betrayal of any one of those is to lose all three."
—Ziad K. Abdelnour

CHAPTER 4

Toastmasters

When I started working with my first firm, CJM Planning Corp, it was necessary for me to speak in front of larger groups of professionals. Having the confidence to execute your thought process and stay on topic is not an easy task. The content was easy enough for me to understand. After all, my knowledge and success as a vice president afforded me the credentials to attract an audience; now, it was up to me to deliver.

My colleague, close friend, and mentor, Paul Thompson, referred me to a group known as Toastmasters. Paul was a selfless man who dedicated his time to the success of others. He knew training and advised me on how to become an effective trainer. At first, I was skeptical about reaching out, but after attending a few meetings, I noted that the ability to present was relevant in every aspect of communicating.

Toastmasters International is a non-profit educational organization operating clubs worldwide to promote communication, public speaking, and leadership skills. Founded in 1924, Toastmasters has grown to have more than 14,000 clubs in 150 countries, with over

270,000 members.[1] Toastmasters offers a structured learning program, Pathways, that consists of six specialized learning paths covering various aspects of communication and leadership.

Toastmasters members can choose paths such as Presentation Mastery and Visionary Communication, Dynamic Leadership, and Persuasive Influence, among others, which guide them through a series of projects and speeches tailored to their goals. Members complete these projects at their own pace, which involves preparing and delivering speeches, conducting research, and developing leadership skills through practical assignments.

Clubs typically meet once a week or bi-weekly. Meetings follow a consistent structure and include prepared speeches, impromptu speaking sessions (Table Topics), and evaluations. Evaluation is a core component of Toastmasters meetings. Members receive feedback on their speeches and performances from peers, focusing on strengths and areas for improvement. This feedback helps members continuously refine their communication and leadership skills. Toastmasters clubs provide a supportive and encouraging environment where members can practice without fear of judgment. This camaraderie fosters personal growth and confidence.

Members gain the confidence and competence needed to excel in various personal and professional settings through structured learning paths, regular practice, constructive feedback, and leadership opportunities.

Toastmasters gives you and other professionals seeking to build confidence and practice in front of live audiences a place to go.

---

1   "A Century of Toastmasters International." Toastmasters International-A Century of Toastmasters International. Accessed March 8, 2025. https://www.toastmasters.org/magazine/magazine-issues/2024/oct/a-century-of-toastmasters-international.

The more you work at it, the more confident you will get

> *I want to share with you some techniques I have used*
> *throughout my career that have helped me with my*
> *communication skills.*

COMMUNICATION-FOSTERING TECHNIQUES

- I start my day and say good morning to as many people as I can, making direct eye contact with everyone.
- I open doors for strangers whenever the opportunity presents itself, whether I am entering an elevator and allowing others to go before me or greeting perfect strangers walking into a building.
- At times, in line at Dunkin' Donuts, I'll buy a cup of coffee for people who might need a little lift to feel better about themselves.
- I offer to help people who obviously need assistance, just by saying, "Can I help in any way?"

One day an elderly woman with a cane was making her way to my office doors. I stood at the door and waited for her to approach so that I could hold it open for her. I thought of my 90-year-old mother and hoped in my heart that someone would do for her what I was doing for this perfect stranger. The woman looked at me and said there was no need for me to wait for her to reach the door. I replied, "Please take your time. I only hope someone will one day do the same for my 90-year-old mom." She smiled at me and said, "I'm 94, and your mother is blessed to have such a thoughtful son." That made my day.

31

Doing small tasks like these is a great way to build confidence in yourself and become part of the human family. Small acts lead to the ability to build character.

"The way we communicate with others and with ourselves ultimately determines the quality of our lives."
—Tony Robbins

CHAPTER 5

Preparing Yourself for a Changing World

As we've discussed, technology and social media, although helpful in many ways, can also cause distractions and disruptions. I urge you to research your ideas and resist falling prey to those intent on manipulating facts to advance their agenda. Ask questions and educate yourself on current events.

Especially in this day and age, when news is different than it used to be and many outlets actively propagandize current events, you must do the work to find the facts. Most 24-hour networks are not newsworthy organizations but are promotional agencies working with political organizations and large advocacy groups intended to promote agendas. Some outlets even proclaim they are "entertainment" to get away with sharing their propaganda. Others simply duck any responsibility of reporting the facts but lean heavily on their agendas to support their true audience—the advertisers paying them to stay on the air.

Just as many media verticals pervert the truth, higher education is under the microscope for promoting their agendas. For this reason, among others, you must do the work to understand the value of higher education and its associated costs. What are you really buying? How valuable is that name chiseled above the quad? Don't feel so pressured to give into the perception that students have a huge advantage by tacking a specific name onto their degrees. You can attain what you hope to educationally, through community colleges providing elective courses at a significantly lower cost.

Universities and colleges are businesses. That is their priority one: to bring in money. Whether they promote themselves as private or public, they are in business to provide an education. Do not allow yourself to be manipulated to buy some worthless degree that, on the surface, may sound well-intentioned but offers no opportunity to provide you with a fulfilling career. Use the educational system to your benefit. Research grants and scholarships and apply to as many different financial resources as possible.

> *I can't tell you the number of students I have heard of who just didn't take the time to do the research to find thousands of dollars in free money. You can invest in yourself at least this much, right?*

You can skip scrolling for a few hours to gain a massive paydown on your student loans. Trust me, your friends and all the doom scrolling will still be there when you are done. But in four years, you will be so thankful you took the time to shave thousands off your loan, resulting in less stressful finances for you!

If college doesn't appeal to you, look for a trade that can provide you with an opportunity to grow. Many openings in the service industry and the trades can provide you with meaningful employment. You don't have to go to college if that is not where your heart is. The trades are not spoken of favorably enough now. But google a little, and you will see the going rates for carpenters, mechanics, and welders, for instance. These are people making a good, sustainable income.

Above all, do something you enjoy. Having employment you're happy with is half the battle. You will look forward to your daily interactions, pursue learning new skills without prompting since your passion will drive you, and meet interesting people who share your interests.

You may not believe me now, but life is short. Take advantage of your time, and always remember, "Today is the last day of the rest of your life." It's an appropriate phrase, especially when we recall the story of what brought about this timeless saying. Back in 1984, a rebellious, punked-out Ulli Lust set out for a wild hitchhiking ride across Italy, from Naples through Verona and Rome, eventually ending up in Sicily. Twenty-five years later, this talented Austrian cartoonist has looked back at that tumultuous summer and delivered a long, dense, sensitive, and minutely observed autobiographical graphic novel masterpiece called *Today Is the Last Day of the Rest of Your Life.*

We should never take time for granted.

It might not surprise you to know that the most successful individuals have mastered the best time management techniques essential for improving productivity and reducing stress. I recommend dividing your tasks into four categories: 1) urgent and important, 2) important but not urgent, 3) urgent but not important, and 4) neither urgent nor important. Focus on the urgent and important tasks first. Everything else can come after that.

Prepare your day, too. Spend a few minutes each morning or the night before planning it out. List the tasks you need to accomplish and allocate time slots for each. Review your goals every Monday, and plan how to accomplish them within that week. Identify the major tasks and deadlines that may prevent you from progressing.

Allocating specific blocks of time to different tasks or activities allows you to focus exclusively on the task at hand. This helps prevent multi-tasking and improves concentration. Staying focused can be challenging, so give yourself little rewards for completing tasks.

Group similar tasks together and perform them in a single block of time. For example, handle all your emails at once, then move on to another type of task. Grouping reduces the mental cost of task-switching. Task-switching is a psychological term that requires doing one task at a time, and it's different than multi-tasking. When you set aside time to work on your tasks and move to the next one and the one after that, and so on, before completing the first, you are task-switching. With this strategy, you will have many uncompleted tasks, but that's okay because you will be progressing on them all versus neglecting or delaying tasks that need to be done more quickly.

I recognize that it's hard to identify, eliminate, or minimize distractions. A few tactics you can take are setting specific times to check emails, using apps to block websites that want to pull your attention, or creating a dedicated workspace free from interruptions. In addition, regularly reviewing your time management strategies and assessing what is working and what isn't will help you nurture these good habits. Be flexible and willing to adjust your approach as needed. Ensure you allocate time for rest, relaxation, and personal activities. A balanced lifestyle supports your overall well-being and sustained productivity.

This is not a one-and-done application. Implementing these techniques requires practice and consistency. When you combine several of these strategies, you can create a personalized approach to time management that maximizes your efficiency and supports your goals.

Your world will change when you are old enough to work. The average person seeks employment of some sort as young as 16 years of age. Doing so can lead to developing communication skills, discipline, and, most importantly, earning money. Nothing is more rewarding than receiving a paycheck after working or being paid to accomplish a task. This is empowerment.

Look, it's no secret that we all get a job to earn money. But we need to look at that job as much more than that. We need to use this opportunity to improve our communication skills, network with colleagues, develop new friendships, *and* earn money.

> *If you take nothing else away from our discussion about money, understand that "money" is a tool. Use it wisely, and invest it to work for you.*

Take the time to comprehend long-term goals and how to budget your money. Creating a strategy and staying on course will only lead to success.

Not having the skill set of what to do with money after it is earned could be devasting. Most people I see spend their money as soon as they get it. After all, money is used to purchase products and services. But how much of your money are you eating in take-out or dine-in food, for instance? How is splurging on material goods that won't pay you back later helping you save and develop the skill set to learn the art of creating wealth? Of course, it's not. You know that. A basic understanding of needs and wants and establishing these fundamentals early on could prove crucial in creating wealth. That's why I want you to apply these lessons early. When you get a head start on building wealth, I can't underscore enough how different your life can be. And you need that more than ever in this changing world.

Needs and wants are fundamental concepts in economics and psychology that help explain human behavior and decision-making.

Needs are essential for human survival and well-being. To be clear, these include physiological requirements such as food, water, shelter, and clothing—not designer clothing. Needs also differ from wants; denying ourselves them is where we get into trouble.

Humans are social beings; thus, they need social connection and belonging. This need encompasses relationships with family, friends, and community, as well as the need for love, affection, and intimacy. Interaction with our peers, in many cases, takes place in social environments. These needs can overlap into a feeling of want, and regardless of how they originated, we might find our purse or wallet lighter than we want them to be if we can't get our impulses under control.

Wants are desires or preferences that go beyond basic needs. Individual tastes, preferences, and aspirations influence them. Wants often include luxuries and comforts that enhance the quality of life (designer clothing, for instance) but are unnecessary for survival— and that we might not be able to afford, or that we think by purchasing categorizes us into a more elite echelon. Wants include luxury goods, entertainment, travel, and leisure activities. Naturally, they involve acquiring material possessions and expensive cars. I think you will agree with me and have experienced, as we all have, that these types of purchases provide short-term enjoyment or satisfaction, but they are not essential for survival.

Wants also extend to experiences and activities that bring pleasure, excitement, or enjoyment, such as dining out at fancy restaurants, attending expensive concerts, or traveling to exotic destinations. Wants can be serious derailers when we don't practice self-discipline and aren't honest about what we can really afford. And it might not be as much fun, but I assure you that you can live on less and move your money to more profitable long-term ventures so that you can *enjoy* it after a time. Crazy but true!

"Too many people spend money they haven't earned to buy things they don't want, to impress people that they don't like."
—Will Rogers

I'm sure I don't have to tell you that discipline is required when setting goals, especially when you are budgeting and learning how to spend money once it is earned. Not having a budget and spending money with no sense of allocation can be wasteful and cause you to fall into debt. But if you catch yourself before falling too far, you can regain your footing and get back on a more profitable track.

Avoiding debt at a young age requires a combination of financial discipline, responsible decision-making, and proactive planning.

You have a higher chance of reaching your optimal financial state if you develop a budget outlining your income, expenses, and savings goals.

Track your spending to ensure you're living within your means and allocate funds for essential expenses, savings, and discretionary spending. Avoid the temptation to spend all your income. Instead, aim to live below your means by prioritizing needs over wants and being mindful of unnecessary expenses. This allows you to save money for emergencies and future goals.

Establish an emergency fund to cover unexpected expenses such as medical bills, car repairs, or job loss (an emergency can kick your financial feet right out from under you, so please heed this advice).

Aim to save three to six months' worth of living expenses in a separate savings account you will not touch unless it is direly required.

While credit cards offer convenience, using them irresponsibly can lead to debt. Limit your use of credit cards and pay off the total balance each month to avoid interest charges. Use cash or debit cards for everyday purchases whenever possible. Research and compare prices, explore financing options, and save for large purchases rather than relying on loans or credit. There's nothing wrong with using coupons or the savings from a store membership, either. Before making a purchase, especially a significant one, consider whether it aligns with your financial goals and priorities. Avoid impulse buying and practice mindful spending by distinguishing between needs and wants.

Invest in your education and skill development to increase your earning potential and career opportunities. And don't forget to research scholarships, grants, and part-time work options to help finance your education without relying heavily on student loans. You want to do everything you can to reduce your debt at an earlier age, which encompasses practicing good habits and seeking out ways to save. Every little bit you don't have to shell out adds up!

Don't hesitate to seek advice from trusted family members, mentors, or financial professionals if you're unsure about financial decisions or facing challenges managing your finances. By adopting these habits and strategies early on, you can establish a solid financial foundation and avoid accumulating debt that can hinder your financial well-being in the long run.

The other option is to ignore discipline and savings. But please don't do this. It's unnecessary and likely will cause you pain that can affect your quality of life, mental wellness, and credit report. As time passes, the adverse effects will also hamper your ability to create wealth and prevent you from establishing a healthy lifestyle.

The overarching message is to determine what is most important to you—career, relationships, personal growth, and leisure—and prioritize these areas to ensure your actions align with your values and goals.

Finally, please know that many of the examples of distractions I covered earlier are designed to manipulate you and give favor to those who wish to create fear and support for their existence through that echo chamber.

It's as simple as popping a balloon. Yet, like that balloon, we often overthink what will cancel this culture. Remember, these unsavory people cannot exist without an audience to inflate the narrative. Don't get sucked in to become a part of that audience. Respect the dynamics of the times we live in, and choose to take care of yourself every day.

"One way to boost our willpower and focus is to manage our distractions instead of letting them manage us."
—Daniel Goleman

CHAPTER 6

Creating Wealth and Achieving Financial Success

Creating wealth as a young person can be an exciting journey filled with opportunities for growth and financial stability. Start by investing in your education and skill development, then continuously seek opportunities to learn new things through formal education, workshops, online courses, or self-study. The more valuable your skills and knowledge, the more opportunities you'll have for higher-paying jobs or entrepreneurial ventures.

Live below your means to avoid lifestyle inflation, especially in the early stages of your career. Instead of spending all your income, prioritize saving and investing a portion. This habit will allow you to build wealth faster and provide a cushion for unexpected expenses or opportunities.

Networking is crucial for both personal and professional growth. So, build relationships with mentors, peers, and professionals in your field who can offer guidance, support, and opportunities.

Networking can open doors to new job opportunities, partnerships, and investment prospects.

When people ask me to name the most influential people in my life, a few names come to mind quickly. I know these people personally, and they have had a direct impact on my life and success: Hank Benvenisti (life coach), Charles Musumeci (founder CJM Financial Services), Paul Thompson (mentor), and Brian O'Toole (CEO AssetMark Investment Services). These individuals have had significant, positive impacts on my life.

Let me tie in a quick story about my eldest son with these influencers. My son attended college to receive his degree in criminal justice. He planned to become a police officer. In New Jersey, this is a great-paying career offering excellent benefits. After graduation, he would interview with many different municipalities to be considered for the police academy. While he waited for his interview results to process, he worked loss prevention for a large retailer. This was a tough time for him as he hated his status.

One day, he explained to me that there was another option to accomplish his career goal—he could pay for police officer training. I agreed to the plan and assisted him with the cost. After six months of training, my son graduated with a police officer certification. His certification would spare any department the cost of training and make his consideration more likely.

The year was 2008, and the US economy was on the brink of a depression. All public hiring was frozen, and any public service hiring was put on hold. After a summer of partying with his friends at the Jersey Shore, I asked my son what his plan was. He gave me multiple excuses. Again, I asked, "So, what is the plan?" He had no response.

It was now time for hard love. I explained to my son that he needed to start networking with people who could give him guidance. Perhaps he could get a full-time job in some other security detail and not rule out a second job at night. I explained to him that hanging out with friends would not advance him in his search, and it was consuming a tremendous amount of his time. In addition, I wasn't going to stand idle and financially support him any longer. It was time to put up or shut up.

My son secured a part-time job as a valet parking attendant. It wasn't about vanity; it was about utilizing his time wisely.

One night, he was parking cars for a political event. His former guidance counselor, now a state assemblywoman, was thrilled to see him and asked what he was doing. He explained his journey and how he was a certified police officer but couldn't find a job. She told him to call her office and set up an appointment. Knowing my son, his education, and his commitment to community and service, she worked to secure him employment as a police officer for New Jersey State Transit Police.

He proudly served as a police officer for seven years while attending Seton Hall University and receiving his master's in public safety. Today, he is a detective in the community where he grew up. I am very proud of his achievements—most importantly, his willingness to stay focused.

The lesson here is "networking." I can't express enough how important it is to network, whether through local groups or professional or volunteer organizations.

Building wealth takes time and requires discipline and patience. Stay focused on your long-term personal and financial goals, and avoid making impulsive decisions based on short-term circumstance changes or peer pressure. Consistency and perseverance are key to achieving personal and financial success over time.

Remember that creating wealth is a journey, and there may be setbacks along the way. Stay adaptable, learn from your experiences, and remain committed to your personal and financial goals. By following these strategies and practicing discipline, you can set yourself on the path to financial independence and long-term wealth accumulation.

Many successful people will share personal stories of working two or three jobs. Jobs are essential for earning a living and often contribute to the economy, personal development, and social structure. As you work on yourself, you can interact with others and, most importantly, make money. Many relationships are formed in a work environment. Colleagues, co-workers, and connections made through employment help build long-lasting life experiences.

Having a part-time job in addition to a full-time job can offer several advantages. Extra earnings from a part-time job can provide a financial buffer, help you pay off debts, save for future goals, or enhance your quality of life. Additional income can significantly boost your savings, preparing you for emergencies. Working in different roles or industries can help you acquire new skills and experiences, making you more versatile and marketable. As a side note, work as much as possible when you are young and before starting your family. This is the time when you aren't encumbered and have the freedom to make as much money as you want while networking and working with people in a symbiotic fashion.

Exposure to various work environments and responsibilities can broaden your professional knowledge and capabilities. A full-time or part-time job can introduce you to new colleagues and professionals, expanding your professional network and potential career opportunities. Managing two jobs can improve your time management and organizational skills as you learn to prioritize tasks effectively. Naturally, having two sources of income can make you more resilient to economic fluctuations and job market changes.

Balancing a full-time and part-time job can be challenging, but it is manageable with proper planning and self-regulation. Plot out your week in advance, allocating specific times for each job, personal time, and rest. Identify high-priority tasks and tackle them first to ensure important deadlines are met. Prioritize sleeping 7-8 hours each night to stay productive and avoid burnout. Maintain a balanced diet and regular exercise routine to keep your energy levels up.

> *When thinking about the ideas that I want to impart to you concerning being efficient and your potential employment choices, Albert Einstein's quote springs to mind: "The only reason for time is so that everything doesn't happen at once."*

I promise that once you start being a little more deliberate with your time, you will uncover more time to do what you love. Time efficiency isn't just about how you operate in the professional world. It can help you gain back lost moments.

Part-time jobs could include something you enjoy. For example, if you like golf, work as a player assistant at a private country club and capitalize on the chance to earn cash tips and network. Similarly, if you enjoy the nightlife, you can work as a bartender, server, host, or hostess in a restaurant.

You could start a side hustle as an Uber or Lyft Driver. With an aging population, many seniors require someone to manage small chores or drive them to medical appointments.

Simply cashiering in a grocery store or working as a service person in a retail establishment can allow you to network and add extra finances, although it won't be as rewarding as doing something you truly love. Remember, whatever you do for work should be enjoyable. It will make your time move much faster as you create and operate from a positive mindset.

You must make sacrifices early on to earn as much money as possible.

And you have the advantage here because of your age and fewer obligations to others who rely on your support as opposed to when you get older. Not to mention, you have the energy to work. Earning money is one of the most rewarding endeavors one can undertake. It is also needed to invest in your future, but you need energy and time to do it properly.

Many people find themselves never earning enough money and think the solution is to work more or harder. Yet the problem is likely a lack of budgeting and affordability. You might tend to spend money foolishly and fulfill desires created by a socially engineered society geared toward satisfying wants. Resist doing this to yourself.

Time is often considered the most crucial element in investing due to the power of compounding interest. The longer the investment period, the stronger the effect of compound interest, which significantly increases returns, especially when dividends are reinvested. Additionally, the volatility of equity returns tends to smooth out over the long run, making time a valuable ally for investors. Understanding your investment time horizon is also critical, as it determines the types of assets you should invest in and the tolerable risk level. The more time you take to access the investment, the more volatility and risk you can withstand, potentially leading to higher returns.

Moreover, investing early can lead to substantial wealth accumulation over time, as has been demonstrated by various scenarios where consistent, long-term investments outperformed those started later, even with the same monthly contributions.

Time in the market, rather than timing the market, is often the best predictor of total investment performance.

Allow time to work for your benefit. The younger you are or the sooner you begin any investment strategy, the more time you will permit yourself for equity investments and the greater your opportunity to create wealth.

"Time is the greatest and most valuable commodity of all . . . It is free."
—Mario Sicari

CHAPTER 7

Understanding the Dollar

Now that you have read a bit about improving yourself for a challenging world, let's talk about money, how it works, and how to leverage it for your benefit.

The US dollar is the official currency of the United States of America and is widely recognized as the world's most dominant primary reserve currency. I'll explain more about what I mean by this, so keep reading. Our dollar serves as the standard currency unit for international trade and financial transactions, and its value is a key indicator of global economic health.

As the US dollar is established as a legal tender within the United States, it is accepted as a valid form of payment for goods, services, and debts. Our government has the authority to issue and regulate the supply of US dollars through the Federal Reserve System, the nation's central bank. Central banks and governments around the globe hold US dollars as part of their foreign exchange reserves, providing stability and liquidity to the global financial system. This status gives the US considerable influence in international finance and trade.

The US dollar is the preferred currency for international trade, particularly in commodities such as oil, gold, and agricultural products. Most international transactions are denominated in US dollars, simplifying trade and reducing exchange rate risks for businesses and governments.

Domestic, global, and institutional Investors often seek refuge in US dollars, known as a "safe haven asset" during economic uncertainty or geopolitical instability.

It's easy to google, but I'll save you the effort and tell you that a "'safe haven asset' is a financial instrument that is expected to maintain or even increase in value during times of economic uncertainty or market turmoil, [and] is often sought by investors to limit their losses when other assets are declining; examples include gold, the US dollar, Swiss franc, and government bonds."

This flight to safety strengthens the dollar's value relative to other currencies and assets, providing stability and liquidity in turbulent times.

The US Federal Reserve's policies, including interest rate decisions, monetary stimulus measures, and quantitative easing programs (QEs involve a central bank buying a large volume of assets to spark economic activity), can significantly influence the value of the US dollar. Interest rate changes, inflation expectations, and economic indicators can impact investor sentiment and the dollar's value in global markets.

> *Foreign exchange markets determine the value of the US dollar relative to other currencies through supply and demand dynamics.*

Fluctuations in exchange rates impact international trade competitiveness, cross-border investments (the practice of investing in companies or projects located in a different country than where the investor is based), and the purchasing power of consumers and businesses, known as inflation. All these factors directly impact the US dollar.

Overall, the US dollar plays a central role in the global economy, serving as a medium of exchange, a store of value, and a unit of account. Its stability, liquidity, and widespread acceptance make it a cornerstone of international finance and trade, influencing economic policies, financial markets, and geopolitical dynamics worldwide.

Understanding this concept helps us comprehend how economies function and how transactions occur within them. Without money, trade would rely on cumbersome barter systems, limiting economic activity and efficiency.

WHAT DOES THIS HAVE TO DO WITH YOUR MONEY?

I say all that to say this: understanding how inflation and other factors can erode the value of money over time enables you to make prudent financial choices. Knowledge of monetary concepts is essential for your effective personal financial management. Understanding budgeting, saving, investing, debt management, and risk mitigation empowers you to make sound financial decisions and achieve your long-term financial goals.

In today's complex world, understanding money concepts is vital for critically evaluating economic policies, financial news, and societal issues. It empowers you to participate in informed discussions about inflation, monetary policy, income inequality, and financial regulation.

TIME VALUE OF MONEY (TVM)

The time value of money (TVM) is a foundational concept in finance and investing that states that money available today is worth more than the same amount of money in the future. Money can earn interest or other returns over time, so the earlier you have it, the more you can do with it—just another reason to focus on building your financial foundation as early as possible.

There are a few key principles behind the time value of money. As noted on Investopedia[2]:

Future Value (FV): Refers to the value of an investment at a specified date in the future, assuming a certain rate of return or interest rate. Essentially, it's calculating what your money will be worth in the future if it's invested or saved.

Present Value (PV): The current value of a future sum of money, discounted at a certain rate of return. It answers the question: "How much is a future amount of money worth today?"

Interest Rates: The rate at which money grows or declines in value over time is crucial in TVM calculations. It could be an interest rate on a savings account, a bond yield, or the expected return on an investment.

Time Period: Time significantly impacts the value of money. Generally, the longer you must wait for a sum of money, the less it's worth today due to the opportunity cost of not having it available for other investments or consumption.

TVM is particularly relevant in investing because it helps investors make informed decisions about the profitability of various investment opportunities. By understanding the time value of money,

---

2   Investopedia. Accessed March 8, 2025. https://www.investopedia.com/.

investors can compare the present value of their investment options and determine which offers the highest potential return for a given level of risk.

For example, if you're considering investing $1,000 in a savings account offering a 5% annual interest rate, understanding TVM allows you to calculate how much that investment will be worth in the future and compare it to other potential investments. Similarly, if you're evaluating whether to take out a loan, TVM helps you assess the total cost of borrowing by calculating the present value of future loan payments.

The time value of money is a fundamental concept in finance that recognizes the importance of cash flow timing. By considering TVM principles, investors can make more informed decisions about saving, investing, borrowing, and lending money.

Understanding these foundational concepts of the dollar, money, and time value is critical when handling basic financial concepts, especially when applying these formulas to borrowing money.

"Time is money, says the proverb, but turn it around, and you get a precious truth. Money is time."
—George Gissing

CHAPTER 8

Understanding Credit

Borrowing money in the form of credit means obtaining funds from a lender with the agreement to pay it back later, often with interest. Credit can take various forms, such as credit cards, loans, lines of credit, or mortgages. Let's look at how it works.

The first step in borrowing is applying for credit with a lender. This could be a bank, credit union, online lender, or credit card company. The lender gauges your creditworthiness, typically assessing your credit history, income, employment status, and other financial factors.

If your application is approved, the lender extends you a line of credit or a specific loan amount.

This amount represents the maximum you can borrow. The lender sets terms and conditions for the credit, including the interest rate, repayment schedule, and any fees associated with the credit.

Once approved, you can use the credit to make purchases, pay bills, or cover other expenses, depending on the type of credit you've obtained. You are required to repay the borrowed amount according to the terms of the agreement. This involves making regular payments, which may be monthly, bi-monthly, or according to another schedule. Each payment includes a portion of the principal amount borrowed and interest charges.

Interest is the cost of borrowing money and is typically expressed as an annual percentage rate (APR). The interest rate can vary depending on factors such as your credit score, type of credit, and prevailing market rates. There's often a credit limit for revolving credit, such as credit cards or lines of credit, which defines the maximum amount you can borrow at any given time. So, yes, you can borrow up to this limit, but exceeding it may result in penalties or fees.

The credit utilization ratio is the amount of credit you use compared to your total available credit. It's a factor in determining your credit score, and lower utilization is generally better for your score. Your repayment history and how you manage your credit obligations can impact your credit score. Timely payments and responsible credit use can improve your score, while late payments or defaulting on loans can damage it.

While credit can provide convenient access to funds, you must recognize the costs and risks involved.

Borrowing money means you must pay it back with interest, and failure to repay as agreed can result in penalties, fees, and damage to your credit score.

Borrowing money can be a useful financial strategy when used responsibly, but it requires careful management to avoid financial difficulties.

Here is a scenario of borrowing $100,000 at 6% interest and paying it back over 30 years:

We typically use an amortization schedule to calculate the repayment plan. This schedule breaks down each payment into two components: interest and principal.

For a 30-year loan with a fixed interest rate, you would make 360 equal payments (30 years x 12 months/year = 360 months).

To calculate the monthly payment, you can use the formula for a fixed-rate mortgage:

Where:

M = Monthly payment

P = Principal amount ($100,000)

R = Monthly interest rate: 6%
  (annual rate divided by 12 months)

N = Total number of payments
  (30 years x 12 months/year = 360 months)

First, we need to convert the annual interest rate to a monthly rate:

R = 0.005 (6% Annual Rate—Expressed as 0.06 / 12 Monthly Payments Per Year.

Then, we can plug these values into the formula to find the monthly payment:

$100,000 / {[(1 + 0.005)^360] - 1} / [0.005 (1 + 0.005)^360]= $599.5

So, your monthly payment would be approximately $599.95

Each month, a portion of this payment would go toward interest and the remainder toward reducing the principal. Over time, the portion of each payment applied toward the principal would gradually increase while the portion going toward interest would decrease. At the end of this scenario, the cost of borrowing **$100,000 @ 6% and paying it over 30 years =$115,838 interest payments + $100,000 Borrowed = $215,838.**

I share this example to give you a concept of the costs of borrowing money. Governments, institutions, and individuals borrow money regularly. When debt exceeds income, as is the case with many governments, institutions, and individuals, the system can lead to financial collapse, bankruptcy, and financial hardship. This is one of the reasons it is so important to understand the responsibility associated with borrowing.

The US debt is the total amount of money the federal government owes to creditors, including individuals, corporations, foreign governments, and other entities who have loaned money to the government by purchasing US treasury securities such as bonds, bills, and notes. This debt accumulates over time as the government spends more than it collects in revenue through taxes and other sources. This is called deficit spending, which just means that more money has been borrowed than was budgeted for.

The US debt-to-revenue ratio is a measure that compares the total outstanding debt of the United States government to its annual revenue or income. This ratio provides insight into the government's ability to manage its debt burden relative to its income-generating capacity.

To calculate the debt-to-revenue ratio, you would divide the total US debt by the annual revenue or income of the federal government. Annual revenue typically includes various sources such as taxes (income taxes, payroll taxes, corporate taxes, etc.), fees, tariffs, and other income.

As of this book's writing, US debt is over $36 trillion.[3] The federal government's annual revenue can vary from year to year due to economic conditions, tax policies, and other factors.

If we assume an annual revenue of around $4 trillion, the US debt-to-revenue ratio would be:

Debt-to-Revenue Ratio = (US Debt) / (Annual Revenue)

$32 trillion / $4 trillion = 8 to 1

This means that for every dollar of revenue the US government generates annually, it has approximately $8 in debt. A higher debt-to-revenue ratio indicates a heavier debt burden relative to the government's income, which can raise concerns about fiscal sustainability and the ability to service the debt.

> *Our current debt ratio is close to the US ratio during World War II, but remember that the world was at war. We are not at war today.*

Imagine for a moment that a person earns a yearly salary of $100,000 and then uses credit to spend an additional $800,000 per year every year. The US Government never had a revenue problem. Through the House of Representatives and the Executive Branch, the US Government has a significant reckless spending problem that will ultimately bankrupt America one day. Every single world empire, from the Roman Empire and the USSR to the Ming Dynasty, has eventually seen its global dominance lead to financial decline.

---

3   "Fiscal Data Explains the National Debt." Understanding the National Debt | U.S. Treasury Fiscal Data. Accessed March 27, 2025. https://fiscaldata.treasury. gov/americas-finance-guide/national-debt/.

THE ART OF CREATING WEALTH

Our political leaders are destroying our currency and wreaking havoc on our economic standing in the world.

> *"Beware of little expenses. A small leak will sink a great ship."*
> —Benjamin Franklin

CHAPTER 9

Exposure to Equity Investments and Account Types

According to the *Federal Reserve's 2022 Survey of Consumer Finances*, about 58% of households own stock in the United States. That's up from 53% in 2019, marking the highest household stock-ownership rate recorded in this triennial survey.[4]

Many of these holdings are reflected through the utilization of company-sponsored retirement accounts, such as 401(k)s and pension plans. Others represent people owning stocks through individual brokerage accounts, where diversification can be achieved through owning shares in mutual funds or index funds.

*1) A diversified portfolio does not assure a profit or protect against loss in a declining market.

---

4   Soni, Aruni. "A Record High 58% of American Households Now Own Stocks." Business Insider. Accessed February 7, 2025. https://markets.businessinsider.com/news/stocks/record-high-american-households-own-stocks-investing-pandemic-markets-money-2023-10

2) Investors cannot invest directly in indexes. The performance of any index is not indicative of the performance of any investment and does not take into account the effects of inflation and the fees and expenses associated with investing.

3) Investing in mutual funds is subject to risk and loss of principal. There is no assurance or certainty that any investment strategy will be successful in meeting its objectives.

> *Investing in stocks can be simplified into a series of steps that make the process more inviting, even for beginners.*

Investment accounts come in various forms and are designed to serve different financial goals, tax considerations, and accessibility needs.

Individual brokerage accounts offer general investing with no tax advantages and funds that can be withdrawn with no penalties. Taxes are paid on dividends, interest, and capital gains. Short-term capital gains are taxed as ordinary income, while long-term gains have lower tax rates.

Retirement accounts such as traditional individual retirement arrangements or Roth accounts offer tax-advantage savings for . . . you guessed it . . . retirement. An IRA offers savings with tax-deferred growth. Contributions may be tax-deductible, and taxes are paid upon withdrawal.

*Income may be subject to local, state, and/or the alternative minimum tax.

The current tax law allows for penalty-free withdrawals at the age of 59 ½, with required minimum distributions (RMDs) to begin at age 73. Don't forget that retirement accounts are long-term investments, and starting at a young age provides significant advantages, such as the power of compounding interest and allowing your money to grow, resulting in a much larger nest egg at retirement. Younger people have the flexibility to invest aggressively and enjoy a tax advantage with their contributions.

*Income may be subject to local, state, and/or the alternative minimum tax.

Roth IRAs also offer retirement savings with tax-free growth; the difference is that contributions are made with after-tax dollars, but qualified withdrawals are tax-free. In addition, contributions can be withdrawn anytime tax-free; earnings can be withdrawn tax-free after age 59½ and meeting the 5-year rule.

*Income may be subject to local, state, and/or alternative minimum tax.

The first Roth IRA five-year rule determines if the earnings (such as investment gains, dividends, and interest) from your Roth IRA are tax-free. To be tax-free, you must withdraw the earnings:

- On or after the date when you turn age 59½
- At least five tax years after the first contribution to any Roth IRA that you own

Check with a tax advisor as to which type of IRA is beneficial for your specific goals.

401(k) plans or employment-sponsored retirement accounts are available through many small businesses. It's up to you if you want to participate, and I highly encourage you to do so. You don't want to have regrets about not planning properly when you get older and don't have enough time to save to take care of yourself and your family. It may seem like an item you can eventually get around to, but you need to prioritize investing in your retirement when you can be more aggressive and earn more.

In most circumstances, enrollment is voluntary, and contributions are pre-tax (traditional) or post-tax (Roth), lowering taxable income in traditional plans. Many plans also allow employers to match contributions up to a certain percentage. This is why anyone employed by a firm or company that offers a 401(k) plan should participate. It's literally free money that you get just for enrolling in their program.

Here's a quick example . . .

*The hypothetical investment results are for illustrative purposes only and should not be deemed a representation of past or future results. Actual investment results may be more or less than those shown. This does not represent any specific product (and/or service).

We'll assume an employee's yearly salary is $60,000 with a matching contribution into their 401(k) of 6% of their salary.

The employer will match the employee's contribution dollar for dollar, meaning that 6% of $60,000 = $3,600. A matching contribution means that both the employee and employer contribute $3,600 at the end of the calendar year, bringing the employee account value to $7,200.

In addition, the plan provides different investment choices for both employee and company contributions. Each plan is designed according to the amount vested, which refers to the process by which an employee earns the right to receive full ownership of certain benefits over time.

The employer has a fiduciary responsibility to the plan and participants to keep the funds safe, avoid conflicts of interest, and, most importantly, provide access to educational information to ensure the employee is updated on the plan's benefits.

Starting with a retirement account, especially if your employer offers a match, is a good first step to setting yourself up for a solid retirement due to the immediate tax benefits and potential employer contributions. Once you've maximized the benefits of your retirement accounts, or if you need more flexibility, consider investing in a taxable account. It's also wise to consult a financial advisor to tailor your strategy to your specific financial goals and circumstances.

It's often beneficial to have both types of accounts. Maximize tax-advantaged accounts first (especially if you get an employer match), then invest additional funds in a taxable account. Both account types are suitable for long-term growth, but tax-advantaged accounts can compound faster due to deferred taxes.

EXAMPLE STRATEGY

Step 1: Contribute to your 401(k) up to the employer match.

Step 2: Maximize contributions to an IRA (traditional or Roth, based on your situation).

Step 3: If you have additional funds, put them into a taxable investment account.

WHAT ARE EQUITY INVESTMENTS?

An equity investment, also known as a cash equity investment, is when an investor buys company shares in the stock market, giving them a stake in the company's performance and potential profits. The investor expects the stock to increase in value through capital gains or dividends, allowing them to sell their shares for a profit. The stock market is not a place you can visit but refers to the trading (some physical, most online) of shares representing the partial ownership of companies. It's not only where businesses raise capital, but it is referred to when assessing the economy's health.

In practice, the term "stock market" often refers to one of the major stock market indexes, such as the Dow Jones Industrial Average or the S&P 500 (Standard & Poor's 500), which represent large sections of the stock market. Because it's hard to track every single company, the performance of these indexes is viewed as representative of the entire market.

The S&P 500 is a stock market index measuring the stock performance of 500 large companies listed on stock exchanges in the US. It is widely regarded as one of the best representations of the US stock market and is a key indicator of the economy's overall health. The index covers a broad range of industries and includes tech industry companies that make up the index.

*All investing involves risk, including the possible loss of principal. There is no assurance that any investment strategy will be successful.

It is market-capitalization-weighted, meaning that companies with larger market capitalizations have a greater influence on the index's performance.

Investors use the S&P 500 as a benchmark to compare their investments' performance. An individual investor can invest in the complete S&P 500 Index in various ways. Many investment companies offer shares in the form of an open-ended mutual fund and/

or index fund, resulting in a fully diversified portfolio reflecting the S&P 500, which may help to reduce market risk exposure.

You might see a news headline stating that the stock market has closed up or down for the day. This often means that stocks within the index have gained or lost value as stock market indexes have fluctuated.

Investors who buy and sell stocks hope to profit from the movement in stock prices.

Companies listed on stock exchanges must be public, meaning their shares are open not just to a select few but that they are traded on stock exchanges and elsewhere. Public companies are subject to many reporting and transparency regulations. Stocks are sold to institutional investors and high-net-worth individuals, but also those with far more modest means, seeking income from a share of the profits, so they can sell the stock later at a higher price or simply have a say in how a company runs.

A stock's price changes based on supply and demand, the company's performance, economic conditions, and other factors that might not seem rational—like "investor sentiment"—all of which must be considered if you're buying or selling shares.

People purchase stocks for many reasons. Some hold onto them, looking for income from dividends. Others might think a stock will rise, so they'll snap it up, trying to buy low and sell high. Still, others might be interested in having a say in particular companies' operations. That's because you can vote at shareholder meetings if you meet the criteria of shares that must be owned. Frequently, when stocks are held for an extended period, their prices can appreciate significantly.

But what is considered an extended period? The answer to that question is based on an individual's preference, but I can confidently say that 10-15 years or longer can be an optimal holding period when purchasing stocks, depending on the investor's situation.

For example:

Consider that XYZ Company has a stock symbol XYZ, and that it stood at $20.10 on June 20th, 2014, before any stock splits (which I will explain later), and that today, the stock may trade at a price of $194.03.

The investment of $10,000 in 2014 @ $20.10 = 497.5 shares purchased.

Today, 497.5 shares x $194.03 = $96,529.96 in value.

As another example, we'll say that ABC Company, with the stock symbol ABC, stood at $16.27 on June 13th, 2014, before any stock splits, and today, the stock may trade at a price of $178.34.

The investment of $10,000 in 2014 @ $16.27 = 614.6 shares.

Today, 614.6 shares x $178.34 = $109,607.77 in value.

---

*This illustration is not a recommendation to purchase these stocks but serves as an educational scenario. Always do your own research, or seek the advice of a professional before investing.

NOW, JUST WHAT IS A STOCK SPLIT?

A stock split is a corporate action in which a company issues additional shares to shareholders. Essentially, the company divides existing shares into new shares. Companies often choose to split their stock to lower its trading price to a more comfortable range for most investors and increase the liquidity of shares.

Most investors are more comfortable purchasing, say, 100 shares of a $10 stock as opposed to 1 share of a $1,000 stock. When the share price has risen substantially, many public companies end up declaring a stock split to reduce it. Although the number of shares outstanding increases in a stock split, the *total dollar value* of the shares remains the same as pre-split amounts because the split does not make the company more valuable.

A company's board of directors can choose to split the stock by any ratio. For example, a stock split may be 2-for-1, 3-for-1, 5-for-1, 10-for-1, 100-for-1, etc. A 3-for-1 stock split means that every 1 share an investor holds equates to 3. In other words, the number of outstanding shares in the marketplace triples.

Most companies will initiate what is commonly called a stock buyback program after a stock split to reduce the number of out-standing shares in the marketplace at the lower share price. When the company purchases its shares in the marketplace, they must be converted into treasury stock and can no longer be issued into the market. This move can also signal to investors that a company feels the cash is better used for shareholders, at once supporting the stock price and providing long-term security for investors.

Buybacks can reduce the number of shares outstanding, which can improve financial ratios and offset share dilution.

Owning stocks can be a huge key to creating wealth; much wealth has been created for individual investors over the long term (10-15 years) historically. Many will argue that real estate or tangible assets are the best investments for wealth creation. Regardless, each strategy requires a well-thought-out process, necessitating a complete analysis of tax and real estate laws. Do your due diligence and make sure you are prepared, then take action to start building your wealth and investments for the long term.

"Don't look for the needle in the haystack. Just buy the haystack!"
—John Bogle (founder of Vanguard Funds)

Mutual Fund Investments

Mutual funds are investment vehicles that pool money from multiple investors to buy a diversified portfolio of stocks, bonds, or other securities. They can be actively managed or passively managed (index funds).

Actively managed mutual funds employ professional managers who aim to outperform the market by selecting securities based on research and analysis. Managers can make tactical adjustments according to market conditions and economic outlooks.

Mutual funds offer various investment strategies, asset classes, and sector investments, which are equity schemes that invest in a specific sector of the economy. These sectors can be utilities, energy, infrastructure, etc.

Actively managed funds generally have higher expense ratios due to management fees and operational costs. No-load mutual funds offer the best investment in fee-adjusted returns. A no-load mutual fund means there are no commissions or fees—or no-load—when buying or selling.

HYPOTHETICAL EXAMPLES OF NO-LOAD MUTUAL FUND FAMILIES

XYZ COMPANY

XYZ Total Stock Market Index Fund (XYZX): Covers a large percentage of the entire US stock market.

XYZ 500 Index Fund (XYZFX): Tracks the S&P 500 Index.

XYZ Total Bond Market Index Fund (XYZTX): Provides broad exposure to US investment-grade bonds.

ABC PRICE GROUP

ABC Price Blue-Chip Growth Fund (ABCX): Focuses on large-cap growth stocks.

ABC Price Equity Income Fund (ABCFX): Targets high dividend-paying companies.

ABC International Stock Fund (ABCTX): Invests in a diversified portfolio of international stocks.

WIDGET COMPANY

Widget 500 Index Fund (WCX): Tracks the S&P 500 index.

Widget Total Market Index Fund (WCFX): Provides comprehensive coverage of the entire US stock market.

Widget US Bond Index Fund (WCTX): Offers exposure to the US investment-grade bond market.

Mutual fund shares are continually issuing new shares as investors purchase shares. A fund family may require a minimal investment to open an account. Many fund families allow an individual to make additional contributions of a fixed amount. The shares are issued as fractional shares.

As illustrated, the choices are very similar, yet the fund families differ and rest on the investor's discretion; they are charged with choosing a particular fund family. Returns of the funds in most circumstances are identical.

*This illustration is not a recommendation to purchase these funds but serves as an educational scenario. Always do your own research, or seek the advice of a professional before investing.

"Never depend on a single income.
Make an investment to create a second source."
—Warren Buffett

Index Fund Investments

Index funds seek to keep pace with market-average returns at minimal cost. Index funds provide broad diversification, reducing specific risks, and are generally more cost-effective due to lower expense ratios and tax efficiency. Long-term investors might prefer index funds for their simplicity and low costs.

> *Using index funds as the core of one's portfolio can help to ensure low-cost, broad-market exposure.*

Strategies intending to capture market opportunities or achieve particular investment objectives may be supplemented with actively managed mutual funds or specialized ETFs (exchange-traded funds). ETFs comprise securities that can be exchanged like stocks.

*Investors should consider the investment objectives, risks, charges, and expenses of the funds carefully before investing. The prospectus contains this and other information about the funds. Contact your financial professional to obtain a prospectus, which should be read carefully before investing or sending money.

HYPOTHETICAL EXAMPLES OF INDEX FUNDS

COMPANY 1 INDEX FUNDS

Product 1 Total Stock Market Index Fund (COMIX)

Index Tracked: CRSP US Total Market Index

CRSP stands for the Center for Research in Security Prices, LLC. The CRSP maintains the most comprehensive collection of security price, return, and volume data for the NYSE, AMEX, and NAS-DAQ stock markets.

Description: COMIX provides exposure to the entire US equity market, including small-, mid-, and large-cap growth and value stocks.

Expense Ratio: 0.04%

Product 1 500 Index Fund (COMFX)

Index Tracked: S&P 500

Description: Tracks the performance of 500 of the largest US companies, representing the S&P 500 Index.

Expense Ratio: 0.04%

Company 1 Total International Stock Index Fund (COMSX)

Index Tracked: FTSE (Financial Times Stock Exchange) Global All Cap ex US Index (multiple indices international investors use to benchmark their investments).

Description: Provides exposure to a broad range of developed and emerging markets outside the US.

Expense Ratio: 0.11%

Company 1 Total Bond Market Index Fund (COMBX)

Index Tracked: Bloomberg Barclays US Aggregate Float Adjusted Index

Description: Offers broad exposure to US investment-grade bonds.

Expense Ratio: 0.05%

COMPANY 2 INDEX FUNDS

Company 2 500 Index Fund (COTFX)

Index Tracked: S&P 500

Description: Similar to Company 1's 500 Index Fund, it tracks the S&P 500.

Expense Ratio: 0.015%

Company 2 Total Market Index Fund (COTIX)

Index Tracked: Dow Jones US Total Stock Market Index

Description: Covers the entire US stock market, providing exposure to a wide array of companies.

Expense Ratio: 0.015%

Company 2 US Bond Index Fund (COTBX)

Index Tracked: Bloomberg Barclays US Aggregate Bond Index

Description: Tracks the performance of the US investment-grade bond market.

---

*This illustration is not a recommendation to purchase these funds but serves as an educational scenario. Always do your own research or seek the advice of a professional before investing.

To see what investment indices track, look up the security's ticker symbol.

Index funds may require higher minimum investment amounts since their shares trade regularly on exchanges. The settlement works the same way as if you purchased shares of stocks. Share purchases of index funds differ from mutual fund shares since the index funds do not continually issue new shares. The shares are traded based on supply and demand. For example, an index fund may own a company's shares on the S&P 500 Index before its initial offering raises funds and closes them. At that point, the funds are traded based on the underlying securities within the funds. Tracking the S&P 500 makes it easy for investors to purchase shares of the stocks within the index without a need to purchase the entire index.

It is crucial to understand the risk associated when purchasing any investment. Mutual and index funds offer prospectuses that outline the risk, past performance, fees, taxes, holdings, and management of the underlying investments. In some cases, index funds may not own underlying securities but are known as leveraged ETFs.

Leveraged ETFs are designed to amplify the returns of an underlying index or benchmark. They aim to track and deliver multiples of the index's performance, typically daily. Leveraged ETFs can provide investors with greater exposure to an index's performance without the need to invest additional capital. Leveraged ETFs present much more risk to the investor since they do not hold individual securities.

Common leverage ratios are 2x (two times) and 3x (three times), meaning these funds seek to double or triple the daily return of their benchmarks. Inverse leveraged ETFs, on the other hand, seek to achieve the opposite of the index's performance, often using leverage (e.g., -2x or -3x). You can make money with market gains or losses.

ETFs use financial instruments such as derivatives (e.g., futures contracts, options, swaps) and debt to achieve the desired leverage. These instruments allow the fund to gain more exposure to the index than the amount of capital invested; they are intended for daily short shifts in the market, primarily used for day-to-day trading, and are generally not chosen as long-term investments.

---

*Exchange-traded funds are sold only by prospectus. Please consider the investment objectives, risks, charges, and expenses carefully before investing. The prospectus contains this and other information about the investment company and can be obtained from your financial professional. Be sure to read the prospectus carefully before deciding whether to invest.

This falls under the scenario of when something sounds too good to be true; it usually is. So why have them? That is a great question. Unfortunately, some market players carry plenty of influence with regulators and allow large investment firms to create investment vehicles available to the public although they carry a significant amount of risk. I stay away from any leveraged investment.

> *Before you invest, always request the prospectus of the fund. It will detail the underlying investment strategy and holdings.*

If the investment does not align with your long-term strategy, avoid it at all costs.

Leveraged ETFs may not be a good option for novice or seasoned investors. They are complicated and require a well-informed investment background. Most leveraged investments are used by large institutional investors, who risk less capital.

> *Due to their low costs, simplicity, and broad diversification, starting with index funds is often a prudent choice for most investors.*

Let me explain: you'll recall that an index fund begins as an open-ended fund while raising capital. The underwriting firm sets its target of how much capital it will raise prior to closing the fund. While raising capital, the underwriting firm will advertise the underlying investments and goal of the index fund. Hence, once the fund achieves its goal, it closes and is traded on the NYSE like a stock. What determines the value of the ETF is not the underlying investments of the fund but the demand by investors willing to purchase it.

The underlying investments will either appreciate or depreciate depending on market conditions. If the value of the underlying investments appreciates, it will spark more demand from the investing public and cause the price of the ETF to increase. If the opposite should occur, meaning the price of the underlying securities declines, the investing public or shareowners will sell the shares, causing the price of the ETF to decline.

Mutual funds can be beneficial for those with specific investment goals or a strong belief in the potential of active management. When making your decision, it's essential to consider your financial goals, risk tolerance, and investment preferences.

"Buy stocks as you would groceries: when they are on sale."
—Christopher Browne

Comparing Diversification and Individual Stocks

Diversification and individual stock ownership are two distinct investment strategies, each with advantages and disadvantages. Here's a detailed comparison to help you understand the key differences and determine which approach might best suit your investment goals and risk tolerance.

Diversification involves spreading investments across various assets (such as stocks, bonds, real estate, etc.) and within those asset classes (across different industries, geographies, and company sizes) to reduce risk. By holding various investments, the negative performance of some assets can be offset by the positive performance of others, thus reducing the portfolio's overall risk. Diversifying can lead to more stable returns over time as the impact of market volatility is mitigated. Problems specific to one company (e.g., management issues, product recalls) are also less likely to significantly impact the overall portfolio.

Investing in individual stocks involves selecting and holding shares of specific companies based on research and analysis. Investing in individual stocks can have lower costs than mutual funds or ETFs, which may have management fees. That said, do *not* view fees as a negative cost. Researching well is optimal in investing.

Individual stock performance can be highly volatile, and the poor performance of one or a few investments can significantly impact a portfolio. Successful stock picking requires extensive research, analysis, and ongoing monitoring, which can be time-consuming. A concentrated portfolio of individual stocks is exposed to higher risk from company-specific events and market volatility.

A balanced approach combining both strategies can provide a well-rounded portfolio that leverages the benefits of diversification while allowing for the potential of high returns from individual stock picks.

"The journey toward achieving goals is an essential part of our human experience. This is a process of self-discovery, growth, and ultimately fulfillment."
—Mario Sicari

Dollar-Cost Averaging

This is my favorite part of investing. Dollar-cost averaging (DCA) creates a systematic practice of investing regardless of market conditions. In all cases, it has proven successful in keeping investors invested over the long term.

I began my first investment with mutual fund dollar-cost averaging at the age of 24. As happens to most individuals and will likely apply to you, I invested a small amount, but as time went on, I increased my monthly contribution. Whether in a retirement or individual non-qualified account, doing so creates discipline and allows time to work in your favor.

---

*Dollar-cost averaging will not guarantee a profit or protect you from loss but may reduce your average cost per share in a fluctuating market.

DEFINING DOLLAR-COST AVERAGING

Dollar-cost averaging is a simple approach to investing, allowing an individual to contribute a constant dollar amount over an extended period regardless of marketplace fluctuations. This practice requires consistency and patience. Over the long term, it can help mitigate market fluctuation risk and average the cost of shares purchased. Let's look at an example:

A $1,200 one-time purchase in January @ $10 per share = 120 shares

Share price 12 months later = $8 x 120 shares = $960

EXAMPLE OF DCA

Month	Share Price	Amt. Invested	Total Shares
January	$10	$100	10
February	$8	$100	12.5
March	$7	$100	14.3
April	$9	$100	11.1
May	$6	$100	16.7
June	$5	$100	20
July	$7	$100	14.3
August	$8	$100	12.5
September	$6	$100	16.7
October	$8	$100	12.5
November	$7	$100	14.3
December	$8	$100	12.5
Totals		$1,200	167.4

As you can see by the illustration, the market share price changes as the volatility changes. Now, let's assume an investor invested $1,200 over 12 months rather than making a one-time purchase. He would accumulate 167.4 shares in December of that same year, making the value 167.4 @$8 = $1,339.20.

*This example does not reflect sales charges or other expenses that may be required for some investments. Rates of return will vary over time, particularly for long-term investments.

The illustration is an example of averaging the cost down in favor of the investor. The average purchase price over 12 months is $1,200 invested/167.4 shares purchased = $7.17 average price per share (for ease of illustration, I have rounded up the fractional shares here).

This technique of investing a small amount of money is a great method. Many people feel investing requires a large sum of money, but this is not the case. For $100 per month and significant time, commitment, and persistence, you can begin your investment journey of attaining personal wealth, building financial security, and achieving long-term goals.

EXAMINING AND PREPARING YOURSELF FOR RISK

As you take your first step to investing, understand your risk tolerance—your ability and willingness to endure fluctuations in investment value. Consider factors such as your age, income, financial obligations, and investment experience.

Define your short-term, medium-term, and long-term financial objectives, such as buying a home, saving for retirement, funding education, or starting a business.

Before investing, ensure you have an emergency fund with enough savings to cover three to six months of living expenses. This fund will act as a safety net in case of unexpected expenses or job loss.

Prioritize paying off high-interest debt, such as that accrued through credit cards, before investing.

The interest rates on these debts are typically higher than potential investment returns, so eliminating them can save you money in the long run.

Familiarize yourself with various investment vehicles, including stocks, bonds, mutual funds, and ETFs. Spread your investments across different asset classes and industries to reduce risk. Remember, diversification helps minimize the impact of any single investment's poor performance.

Adopt a long-term perspective when investing. Historically, markets have trended upward over time despite short-term downward trends. Avoid trying to time the market or reacting impulsively to market volatility. The power of compounding works best over time. Start investing as early as possible and contribute regularly to your investment accounts to take advantage of compound growth.

Utilize tax-advantaged accounts such as 401(k)s, IRAs, and Health Savings Accounts (HSAs) to minimize taxes and maximize your investment returns. Take advantage of tax-loss harvesting and other tax-efficient investment strategies.

Review your investment portfolio regularly to ensure it remains aligned with your financial goals and risk tolerance. Rebalance your portfolio periodically to maintain your desired asset allocation.

Continuously educate yourself about investing principles, market trends, and economic indicators. Stay informed about changes in your investments and the broader financial landscape.

Investing in personal wealth requires discipline and patience. Stick to your investment plan and remain focused on your long-term objectives.

Investing in personal wealth is a journey that requires careful planning, discipline, and patience. By setting clear goals, understanding your risk tolerance, diversifying your portfolio, and staying informed, you can build a solid foundation for financial success. Remember that investing involves risks, and there are no guarantees of returns. However, a well-thought-out strategy and a long-term perspective can allow you to increase your chances of achieving your financial goals and building wealth over time.

Different asset classes come with varying levels of risk when investing. Stocks offer a high degree of risk, can be volatile, and are influenced by market fluctuations, economic conditions, and company performance. They offer the potential for high returns and the risk of significant losses.

Bonds offer a moderate degree of risk and are generally less volatile than stocks. They provide fixed interest payments and return the principal at maturity, but they can still be subject to credit risk (the issuer might default) and interest rate risk (bond prices fall when interest rates rise).

Mutual funds/ETFs offer various risks and pool money from multiple investors to invest in diversified portfolios of stocks, bonds, or other assets. Risk depends on the fund's specific investments, but diversification can help mitigate individual asset risk.

Real estate investments can provide steady income and capital appreciation. However, they are subject to market conditions and property management issues and can be less liquid than stocks or bonds.

Investments like savings accounts, money market funds, and Treasury bills are considered low-risk and offer lower returns. They are highly liquid and have a minimal risk of loss.

Each type of investment carries its own set of risks and potential rewards. Diversifying across different asset classes can help manage overall risk.

Non-market risk, also known as unsystematic risk, refers to risks specific to a particular company or industry—not the market. For example, you might invest in an oil company while the price of oil is dropping due to supply and demand. Although the price of oil dropping may not present a direct risk to the overall market, it may have an adverse impact on companies in the oil sector, resulting in a lower share price.

*An investment in the fund is neither insured nor guaranteed by the Federal Deposit Insurance Corporation or any other government agency. Although the fund seeks to preserve your $1.00 per share, it is possible to lose money in the fund.

Credit risk, the risk that a borrower will default on their financial obligations, leads to losses for the lender or investor. This is particularly relevant for bonds and loans.

Operational risk is the risk of loss resulting from inadequate or failed internal processes, people, systems, or external events. Examples include fraud, system failures, or natural disasters.

Consider also regulatory risk, the risk of financial loss due to changes in laws or regulations that affect a company or industry. This can include new regulations, legal disputes, or changes in tax policies. This could lead a company into liquidity risk, the risk that an investor cannot buy or sell an investment quickly without significantly affecting its price. This is especially relevant for less liquid assets like real estate or certain small-cap stocks. There is also event risk, which is the risk of a major event affecting the company, such as a merger, acquisition, natural disaster, or major technological change. These events can significantly impact a company's operations and stock price.

Finally, there are political, geographical, social, and mainstream media risks. These risks are often mitigated over short periods. They are real in that they can change investors' sentiments quickly and, more times than not, wreak havoc on portfolios, causing investors to react.

> *Keep reading to learn about the national debt, inflation, and the ins and outs of buying real estate. I do consider real estate an investment, but it brings with it specific considerations, and so it warrants its own chapter. I think you will enjoy it!*

"Security is mostly superstition.
Avoiding danger is no safer in the long run than outright exposure.
Life is either a daring adventure or nothing."
—Helen Keller

CHAPTER 10

Understanding the National Debt, Government Deficits, and the Impact on Citizens

This chapter aims to make you aware of the impact of the dysfunctional spending in Washington and how it affects the economy, inflation, and the people the legislative and executive branches of government are appointed to serve.

As I explained in an earlier chapter, the total amount of money a country's government has borrowed is called its national debt. The components of the national debt are public debt, intergovernmental holdings, such as the Social Security Trust Fund, and money borrowed from foreign governments. The national debt is usually measured as a ratio of GDP (growth domestic product) to the rate at which our economy grows.

"Blessed are the young, for they shall inherit the national debt."
—Herbert Hoover

Federal, state, and local government deficit occurs when a governing body spends more money than it receives in revenue each year. The budget deficit is the difference between expenditures and revenues. To fund their shortfalls, different government entities issue debt securities and borrow money. While this can apply to many entities, we will focus on the federal government in this section.

DEFINING DEFICITS

There are two types of deficits: fiscal deficits and primary deficits. Fiscal deficits are the total amount the government has borrowed to compensate for revenue insufficiencies. Primary deficits comprise interest on past borrowing.

Borrowing for infrastructure, education, and technology can stimulate economic growth. However, this attempt to stimulate growth is usually a non-starter (an initiative that has no chance of succeeding) and only increases GDP for a short period of time. The negative impact is high debt, which can lead to increased taxes or reduced public services if the government needs to pay off debt.

If the government finds itself in a pickle and prints more money to pay off debt, it can lead to high debt levels and potential inflation, reducing purchasing power. This is our current administration's cycle due to the unintended aftermath of the COVID-19 pandemic when the government took measures to mitigate the negative effects of economic closures.

High debt levels might also force cuts in government services or social programs and possibly result in politicians being ousted from office due to the negative impact on voters who rely on government programs for sustainability. It can lead to economic instability and reduced investor confidence, weakening currency and becoming another cause of inflation.

*The consequences of an unstable currency and high debt are
market forces seeking to replace the US dollar with other
forms of currency, such as precious metals and cryptocurrency.*

TAXES

Creating a stable economy for all citizens is not achievable through
tax warfare, regardless of arguments from those who see taxation as
a tool intended to have wealthier individuals sustain the spending
of programs created by the government. The tax system in the US is
complex, and while many legislators have argued wealthy individuals
do not pay taxes due to the tax system, this is a mostly false statement
and an argument used to create class warfare.

Individuals in the workforce are subject to a completely different
tax structure, as are those who do not work and have sustainable
wealth through different means.

Employed individuals are subject to FICA (Federal Insurance
Contributions Act) taxes—payroll taxes that fund Social Security
and Medicare programs in the US. These taxes are imposed on both
employers and employees. In total, and at the time of this writing, employees pay 7.65% of their wages toward FICA taxes, and
employers match this amount, contributing an additional 7.65%.
Self-employed individuals pay both the employee and employer por-
tions, totaling 15.3%, but they can deduct the employer portion
when calculating their income taxes.

*The US federal government levies federal income taxes on
the annual earnings of individuals, corporations, trusts, and
other legal entities.*

These taxes are a significant source of revenue for the government and fund various public services and programs. Taxes are paid by everyone who files a tax return (including employed individuals) and are not to be confused with FICA.

The US federal income tax system is progressive, meaning that tax rates and brackets increase with higher levels of income. An individual is assigned to a specific tax rate applied to income within a tax bracket. Taxpayers file their taxes based on their filing status, such as single, married filing jointly, married filing separately, head of household, or qualifying widow(er). Filing status affects the tax brackets and standard deductions applicable to the taxpayer.

Taxpayers can reduce their taxable income through deductions (e.g., standard deduction or itemized deductions) and tax credits (e.g., child tax credit, earned income tax credit). Deductions lower the income subject to tax, while credits reduce the tax liability directly. Employers withhold federal income tax from employees' paychecks throughout the year based on the information the employee provided on Form W-4. Self-employed individuals and others who do not have taxes withheld may need to make estimated tax payments quarterly.

Some states impose an additional tax on earnings and income, and residents are required to file a state income tax return. Large cities may have a city income tax in addition to state and federal income taxes. The US tax system is intricate; simplification and an overhaul would require time and extreme will from Congress.

To fully understand the ins and outs of the US tax system, conduct your own research. The information in this book provides a basic understanding. Getting more detailed is simply beyond the scope of this book. This is why tax professionals are so busy around tax season!

CAPITAL GAINS TAX AND INTEREST TAX

In addition to income and FICA taxes, tax filers are also subject to capital gains tax when a qualifying situation arises. A capital gains tax is a tax imposed on the sale of an asset. At the time of the writing of this book, the long-term capital gains tax rates for the 2024 and 2025 tax years are 0%, 15%, or 20% of the profit, depending on the filer's income. These taxes are due only after an investment is sold.

Capital gains taxes apply solely to capital assets, which include stocks, bonds, digital assets like cryptocurrencies and NFTs, jewelry, coin collections, and real estate. Long-term gains are levied on investment profits held for more than a year. Short-term gains are taxed based on an individual's regular income tax rate, which is higher than the tax on long-term gains. Capital gains tax doesn't apply to unsold investments or unrealized capital gains (profits on investments or assets that haven't been sold yet but have increased in value).

Most taxpayers pay a higher rate on their income than on any long-term capital gains they may have realized. That gives them a financial incentive to hold investments for at least a year, after which the tax on the profit decreases. The profit on an asset sold less than a year after it is purchased is generally treated as wages or salary for tax purposes. Such gains are added to your income on a tax return.

Capital investments can yield income through capital gains, dividends, and interest. Each year, investors pay taxes on interest from bonds, mutual funds (CDs), and savings accounts. Some interest types are fully taxable, while others are partially taxable. Taxable interest is taxed just like ordinary income.

Dividend income, such as qualified dividends, may be subject to long-term capital gains rates based on the taxpayer's income level and length of holding. Dividends are paid from a company's after-tax income, while interest is paid from pre-tax income. Companies that pay dividends face double taxation: once on their profits and again on the dividends they pay to shareholders. Alternatively, interest payments are tax-deductible and more favorable for companies, as they can lower tax liability.

Investors aim to save money by utilizing tax-efficient tactics to generate dividends, capital gains, or interest. Regardless of its form, it's all considered income, and taxpayers must report it along with any other income sources received during the tax year.

As described, the US tax system is the most complex in the world. In most instances, individuals need a CPA (certified public account) to assist in filing their taxes every year.

No free country has ever taxed its way to prosperity. Prosperity is achieved through a free-market capitalist structure, in which the government participates only as a referee, setting up guidelines businesses can operate under with specific and limited regulations. In doing so, small businesses and corporations can provide needed employment for people to work and earn income.

I'll say it again: the US does not suffer from a revenue problem. The legislative and executive branches of government have severe spending problems resulting from a lack of term limits for elected officials who use their skills to promise constituents an endless stream of benefits funded through government programs—but rarely deliver.

"To preserve our independence, we must not let our rulers load us with perpetual debt. We must make our choice between economy and liberty or profusion and servitude."
—Thomas Jefferson

CHAPTER 11

Why Inflation Happens

DEMAND-PULL INFLATION

Inflation occurs when the demand for goods and services exceeds the supply. This is known as demand-pull inflation, and it can happen due to strong consumer spending, government spending, or investment.

COST-PUSH INFLATION

Cost-push inflation arises when the costs of production increase, leading producers to raise prices to maintain their profit margins. Causes of cost-push inflation include rising wages, higher import prices, or increases in the prices of raw materials.

BUILT-IN INFLATION

Built-in inflation occurs when expectations of future inflation become embedded in wage and price-setting behavior. For example, if workers expect prices to rise, they may demand higher wages, leading to wage-price spirals.

MEASURING INFLATION

Inflation is typically measured using various price indices, such as the Consumer Price Index (CPI) and the Producer Price Index (PPI). These indices track changes in the prices of a basket of goods and services over time. Central banks and governments monitor inflation closely to gauge the economy's health and make policy decisions.

THE POSITIVES AND NEGATIVES OF INFLATION

Although inflation mainly gets a bad rap, we must understand its positive and negative impacts—and yes, *there are* positive impacts!

Inflation can redistribute wealth for both savers and borrowers. Savers may see the real value of their savings eroded, while borrowers may benefit from repaying loans with less valuable currency. High or unpredictable inflation can create uncertainty, making it difficult for businesses and consumers to plan.

Central banks often use interest rates to control inflation. Higher inflation may lead to higher interest rates, which can affect borrowing, investment, and economic growth.

During the COVID-19 pandemic, the US government, through the actions of the US Treasury Department, passed emergency measures intended to keep the economy from falling into a steep decline.

Without knowing the scope of the infection, health officials forced businesses to close unless they were deemed essential. Schools closed and began to work remotely. The overall economy slowed drastically in six short months. Yet, people still needed a source of income. Congress passed immediate bills to provide workers with emergency funds.

Because of this epidemic, since 2019, the US government has added $1 trillion of borrowed funds to its budget to fuel the economy. This action had the unintended consequences of inflation, meaning more dollars were printed, borrowed, and provided to the economy, cheapening the currency's value. In short, more currency infused into the economy caused its value to shrink.

It's important to note that the US' current inflation rate is a direct result of the government stimulus used during the COVID-19 pandemic. The pandemic's unintended consequences, high cash infusion rates into the economy, and a drastic drop in productivity led to double-digit inflation. Inflation can affect a country's competitiveness in international trade. If domestic prices rise faster than those of trading partners, exports may become more expensive, leading to a decline in competitiveness.

MODERATE INFLATION

Central banks typically target low and stable inflation (more commonly known as moderate inflation). This allows for adjustments in relative prices and encourages economic activity.

HYPERINFLATION

Hyperinflation is extremely high and uncontrollable. It is often characterized by rapidly rising prices, collapsing currency values, and economic chaos. It can result from excessive money creation, possibly due to government mismanagement or a loss of confidence in the currency.

While some inflation levels are considered normal and desirable for a healthy economy, excessive inflation can harm economic stability, consumer purchasing power, and overall prosperity. This is why central banks and governments implement various policies to manage inflation and maintain price stability.

WHAT'S POLICY GOT TO DO WITH IT?

Fiscal policy governs decisions regarding spending, taxation, and borrowing. Its effects on inflation are indirect and can vary based on the timing, magnitude, and nature of the fiscal actions taken. Increased government spending can stimulate economic demand, especially for goods and services. If this demand outpaces supply, it can lead to upward pressure on prices, contributing to inflation.

Tax cuts can put more money in consumers' pockets, increasing their purchasing power and potentially driving up demand. Conversely, tax hikes can reduce disposable income and dampen consumer spending, which might alleviate inflationary pressures.

WHY WE'RE IN OUR CURRENT PICKLE

Running large budget deficits (spending more than what's collected in taxes) can lead to increased government borrowing. If the government borrows from the central bank (monetizing the debt), it can increase the money supply, potentially fueling inflation.

In 2019, the government saw the need to spend an additional $4.6 trillion to offset adverse impacts due to the pandemic and the shuttering of the economy.[5] Yet even after the pandemic officially ended, the government did not reduce its spending to pre-COVID

---

5   Office, U.S. Government Accountability. "Covid-19 Relief: Funding and Spending as of Jan. 31, 2023." COVID-19 Relief: Funding and Spending as of Jan. 31, 2023 | U.S. GAO. Accessed March 28, 2025. https://www.gao.gov/products/gao-23-106647.

levels. This increase in spending has led to large budget deficits and a ballooning national debt.

> *Fiscal policies promoting productive investments in infrastructure, education, or technology can enhance long-term economic capacity, potentially mitigating inflationary pressures by expanding supply.*

Many political leaders will argue that the government's role in spending—reckless spending (in most eyes)—combined with no accountability has led to the crony capitalism now plaguing our system.

"The first panacea for a mismanaged nation is inflation of the currency; the second is war. Both bring temporary prosperity; both bring a permanent ruin. But both are the refuge of political and economic opportunists."
—Ernest Hemingway

CHAPTER 12

Property—A Building Block to Your Wealth Foundation

Buying real estate, whether for personal use or investment purposes, can be a major financial decision and requires you to weigh several benefits and risks. For the most part, real estate ownership comes with a tremendous responsibility and cost.

Many individuals view homeownership as a necessity, especially when it comes to raising a family. Location, public schools, recreational opportunities, and neighborhoods will likely be considerations when shopping for a home. These criteria increase the cost of homes within certain communities. An individual must also consider the costs associated with buying a home, such as borrowed funds, a mortgage, taxes, and insurance for the property.

Some individuals who want to own a home may start small, perhaps owning a co-op (cooperative) before a single-family home. A co-op is a unique form of property ownership in which a corporation owns a building or a group of properties. Instead of buying an individual property, such as a condo or single-family home, residents purchase shares in the co-op corporation, entitling them to occupy a specific unit in the building.

Others may decide to own a townhome or condominium. A townhome is a multi-story, attached property where the owner holds both the interior and exterior (land) of the unit. Typically, townhomes share walls with adjacent units. A condominium is a property where you only own the interior space of your unit, while the rest (exterior walls, roof, and common areas) are shared and maintained by a condo association.

In addition to the fixed cost associated with these types of properties, townhomes, condominiums, and co-ops are subject to an additional management cost charged by their associations. This cost may increase year over year depending on the fiscal responsibility of the boards that oversee the management of these properties.

In most cases these properties make more sense for older people who have entered their golden years. The responsibility of property maintenance is reduced, and some properties are even known as over-55 communities—so titled because the age of residents is limited to those over 55.

> *Some first-time homebuyers will consider the purchase of a multi-family home. I purchased my first home with my brother, splitting the cost between the two of us.*

We lived in a two-family house for five years, saved money, and built equity. If you are considering a home purchase, you do not need to enlist a family member or follow anyone else's plan; this was my personal journey. If you like the idea of having a multi-family home, you can always rent the second unit—allowing you to offset the cost associated with the property.

My son lives in a 2-family home. His goal is to acquire other multi-family homes and become a landlord. If he did this, he would own investment properties, which are not just limited to multi-family homes, by the way. Real estate investors can also venture into commercial real estate. For the purposes of our discussion, we will focus on you and your journey. I just want you to understand that there are many resources to allow you to become involved in the complexities of real estate investment.

Before you purchase real estate, decide what the purpose of your investment is. Are you obtaining the property for personal use, or is it investment-related? Investment properties require a commitment of time and work. Is that something you wish to undertake?

For instance, when the tenant has an issue with the unit you are renting, guess who they're going to call (and it's not Ghostbusters)? It's you. So be prepared, and know that call can come at any time. You are the responsible party for assuring the tenants' unit is in full working order and safe.

If you decide to live in a suburban neighborhood and look for an older home that requires some updates, enlist the services of a contractor prior to purchase to inspect the construction of the home and ensure the electrical, plumbing, and structure are in good condition. The roof, heating, and bathrooms may require more intensive and extensive upgrades. It's one thing to paint a few walls; it's another to have to pay for the cost and manage the intricacies of a full renovation.

When you finally decide to own real estate, seek the assistance of a CPA, financial planner, or financial counselor to review your options. You will want to figure the size of your downpayment, mortgage amount, interest rate, and finally, what your budget will be.

The advantage of home ownership is tremendous. In today's market, many folks have profited significantly from homeownership. That should not be the goal.

As of the writing of this book, America is experiencing a housing shortage, spurring many contractors to move away from building individual homes and focus on building apartment complexes, townhomes, and gated communities. This business model is more profitable for them.

Lower interest rates have contributed to higher home prices because more people can afford homes, which increases the demand for housing. As interest rates increase, it slows the availability of money to the public, causing home prices to stabilize and fall. Seek a balance of a sufficient downpayment, a good mortgage rate, and an affordable carry cost.

Applying for a mortgage may also present a challenge. Many factors will determine the rate at which a bank will lend money. Credit history, work history, income, assets, and size and scope of the purchase all factor into whether you can qualify for a purchase.

I believe, at some point, that everyone should set a goal of owning a home. As our aging population becomes more inclined to migrate to warmer and less congested areas, more homes in certain areas of the country will become available. Knowing what you can expect in every stage leading up to homeownership and having sufficient funds to begin the process should be your first steps.

Creating wealth through saving a portion of your earnings and beginning as soon as you earn a paycheck can make the dream a reality. As I have mentioned throughout this book, time is your greatest asset. Don't waste it.

"Ninety percent of all millionaires became so through
owning real estate."
—Andrew Carnegie

CHAPTER 13

Geopolitical Challenges

The geopolitical challenges we face in this country are based on our type of government. In this chapter, we will talk about our current system and other countries' systems. But let's begin with our home turf.

CAPITALISM

America is the land of free market capitalism, often referred to simply as capitalism. It is an economic system characterized by private ownership of the means of production—such as factories, land, and resources—and the operation of markets with minimal government intervention.

In a free-market capitalist system, economic decisions such as what to produce, how to produce, and who to produce for are primarily determined by buyers' and sellers' interactions in competitive markets, guided by the forces of supply and demand. A few examples are:

- A restaurant deciding what types of foods it will offer, where it will run its business, and what it will charge for its meals.

- When Henry Ford decided to build the future of the Ford Motor Company, he did so based on his industrious vision. After he built the factory, his cars proved to be the number one product people wanted to own. However, this did not prevent competitors like Chrysler or Chevrolet from entering the market. Then because of our capitalist system, the consumer decided which vehicle they wanted with no interference from the government.

SOCIALISM

Socialism is a socio-economic system characterized by collective ownership and control of the means of production, distribution, and exchange. In a socialist society, the state, the community, or worker cooperatives own and manage the means of production and resources rather than private individuals or corporations.

EVERYONE'S GOT A PROBLEM . . . NO ONE HAS A SOLUTION

Socialists complain that capitalism leads to unfair and exploitative concentrations of wealth and power in the hands of the relative few who emerge victorious from free-market competition—people who then use their wealth and power to reinforce their social dominance. Because such people are rich, they can choose where and how to live, and their choices, in turn, limit the options of the poor.

In the capitalist example above, Henry Ford's vision would have been mitigated by his being forced to share his wealth through redistributions to others, despite the risk of capital he would have been subject to, even though his ideas were his own.

Debating free market capitalism versus socialism in America is a complex task as it involves contrasting two distinct economic systems with their merits and flaws. In the context of America, this debate often revolves around finding the right balance between individual freedom and social welfare.

Critics of capitalism point to issues such as income inequality, corporate dominance, and insufficient social services. In contrast, fault-finders of socialism raise concerns about government overreach, inefficiency, and the potential for stifling innovation and economic growth.

In truth, the optimal economic system for America will likely involve elements of capitalism and socialism tailored to address the country's unique social and economic challenges. Yet political agendas and lawmakers leaning on their individualist platforms push for their ideologies. One's opinion usually depends on the side they are following. People usually find that making the argument rooted in their opinion is the equivalent of forcing someone who enjoys cold weather to live in a hot tropical climate.

Let's more closely examine the merits and benefits of free-market capitalism.

KEY FEATURES OF CAPITALISM

Private Property Rights: Capitalism emphasizes the importance of private property rights, where individuals and businesses have the legal right to own, use, and dispose of property, including land, resources, and assets. These rights encourage investment, innovation, and entrepreneurship by allowing individuals to benefit from their efforts and take risks with the expectation of earning profits.

Market Competition: Competitive markets are central to capitalism, as they allocate resources efficiently by matching supply with demand. In a competitive market, multiple buyers and sellers freely interact to determine prices and quantities of goods and services.

Competition incentivizes producers to improve quality, innovate, and offer goods and services at competitive prices, leading to greater efficiency and consumer choice.

Limited Government Intervention: Unlike socialist or mixed economies, where the government plays a more active role in regulating and directing economic activity, capitalism advocates for minimal government intervention in the economy. Government involvement is typically limited to enforcing property rights, contracts, and laws to ensure market competition. It strives to prevent fraud and provide for public goods and services that the private sector may underprovide.

Profit Motive: In capitalism, the pursuit of profit is the primary incentive for individuals and businesses to engage in economic activities. Profit signals to producers where consumers value resources most, guiding investment decisions and resource allocation. By seeking to maximize profits, businesses are incentivized to allocate resources efficiently, innovate, and adapt to changing market conditions.

Consumer Sovereignty: Capitalism emphasizes consumer sovereignty, giving consumers the freedom to choose among competing goods and services based on their preferences and purchasing power. Producers respond to consumer demand by producing goods and services that satisfy consumer preferences, leading to a wide variety of products and services tailored to diverse consumer needs and preferences.

While free market capitalism has been associated with economic growth, innovation, and prosperity in many countries, critics argue that it can lead to income inequality, market failures, and social and environmental externalities if left unchecked. Some are also concerned about the impact of industrialism on the environment and, consequently, society.

When America unleashed its industrial revolution, mining and lumber industries created a demand for resources. Roads and railways needed to be constructed, and land was taken from Native Americans at the cost of lives and cultures.

Therefore, debates persist about how to strike the appropriate balance between free market principles and government intervention to enable economic efficiency, equity, and sustainability.

Now, let's put socialism under the microscope.

KEY FEATURES OF SOCIALISM

Collective Ownership: Socialism advocates for the collective ownership of key economic resources rather than private ownership. This can take various forms, including state ownership, where the government controls the means of production, or worker ownership, where workers collectively own and manage enterprises.

Economic Planning: Socialist economies often involve centralized economic planning to coordinate production and distribution. Central planning authorities, such as government agencies or socialist parties, may determine production targets, allocate resources, and set economic prices. This contrasts with market economies, where prices and production decisions are primarily determined by supply and demand in competitive markets.

Redistribution of Wealth: Socialism typically emphasizes the redistribution of wealth and income to promote greater equality and social justice. This may involve progressive taxation, welfare programs, and public services funded through taxation, aiming to provide essential goods and services to all citizens and reduce socio-economic disparities.

<u>Social Ownership of Services</u>: In addition to the means of production, socialists often advocate for the social ownership and provision of essential services such as healthcare, education, transportation, and housing. The goal is to ensure universal access to these services based on need rather than the ability to pay and to prevent their provision from being driven solely by profit motives.

<u>Democratic Control</u>: Some forms of socialism advocate for democratic decision-making processes within the economy and society. These can include worker participation in management decisions, democratic planning mechanisms, and political systems that prioritize public participation and accountability.

It's important to note that socialism has various interpretations, ranging from democratic socialism to more authoritarian forms. Additionally, how socialist principles have been implemented has varied widely across countries and historical contexts, leading to diverse outcomes and experiences.

Critics of socialism often argue that excessive government control can lead to inefficiency, lack of innovation, and infringement on individual liberties. Proponents, on the other hand, argue that socialism can promote social justice, reduce inequality, and ensure that economic activity serves society's needs rather than the interests of a privileged few.

Whether there has ever been a "successful" socialist country is subject to interpretation and debate. Success can be defined in various ways, and the implementation of socialism has varied greatly across different countries and historical contexts. However, there are examples of countries that have adopted socialist policies or experimented with socialist principles to varying degrees.

SOCIALIST COUNTRY EXAMPLES

<u>Nordic Countries (Denmark, Sweden, Norway, Finland)</u>: Often cited as examples of successful social democracy rather than strict socialism, Nordic countries have robust welfare states with high levels of public services, progressive taxation, and strong social safety nets. While they maintain market economies, they also have extensive government involvement in providing healthcare, education, and social services. These countries consistently rank highly on measures of social well-being, including education, healthcare, income equality, and overall quality of life.[6]

<u>Cuba</u>: Since the Cuban Revolution in 1959, Cuba has pursued a socialist system with state ownership and central planning of the economy, along with extensive social welfare programs. Despite facing economic challenges exacerbated by trade embargoes and isolation, Cuba has achieved notable successes in healthcare and education. The country has a high literacy rate, universal healthcare, and a healthcare system that has received international recognition for its achievements.[7]

<u>China</u>: Following the creation of the People's Republic of China (PRC) in 1949, China adopted a socialist system with state ownership of key industries and central planning of the economy. However, since the late 1970s, China has undergone significant economic reforms that introduced elements of market capitalism while retaining one-party rule by the communist party. This hybrid system, often referred to as "socialism with Chinese characteristics," has led to rapid economic growth and lifted millions of people out of poverty,

---

6   "Nordic Countries." Wikipedia, March 1, 2025. https://en.wikipedia.org/wiki/Nordic_countries.

7   "Cuba." Wikipedia, March 6, 2025. https://en.wikipedia.org/wiki/Cuba.

but it has also resulted in significant income inequality and concerns about political freedom.[8]

Kerala, India: Kerala, a state in southern India, has implemented socialist-inspired policies that focus on social welfare, healthcare, education, and land reform. Despite being part of a predominantly capitalist country, Kerala has achieved notable successes in human development indicators, including high literacy rates, low infant mortality, and life expectancy levels comparable to those of developed countries.[9]

Remember that "successful" can be subjective and depends on the criteria for evaluating a country's performance. While some socialist-inspired policies have produced positive outcomes in certain areas, they have also faced challenges and limitations. Some of these challenges and limitations include slow economic growth, less entrepreneurial opportunity and competition, and the lack of motivation of individuals due to anticipated lesser rewards.

We know that complex government intervention has burdened economic growth through excessive regulations. In some instances, regulations offering protection for society prove to have the opposite effect, resulting in higher costs for goods and services. The unintended consequence is slower economic growth, which in turn lowers tax revenue for government services.

Less competition results in substandard products and services. Why would anyone be interested or incentivized to create a better mouse trap?

In the wrong environment, would Steve Jobs have spent countless years developing the smartphone?

---

8   "China." Wikipedia, March 4, 2025. https://en.wikipedia.org/wiki/China.

9   "Kerala." Wikipedia, March 8, 2025. https://en.wikipedia.org/wiki/Kerala.

The debate over socialism's effectiveness continues to be complex and contentious in economic and political discourse.

CRONY CAPITALISM

There is another segment of capitalism to be aware of. "Crony capitalism" refers to a system in which businesses and individuals with close relationships with government officials or politicians receive preferential treatment and benefits over others in the market. In crony capitalism, these favored entities often gain advantages such as subsidies, tax breaks, regulatory exemptions, and government contracts not because of their merit or efficiency but because of their connections to those in power.

Crony capitalism involves collusion between government officials and certain businesses or individuals to advance their mutual interests. This collusion can take various forms, including regulatory capture (where regulators act in the interest of the industries they are supposed to regulate, leading to lax enforcement of rules and regulations), lobbying for favorable legislation or regulations, and awarding government contracts to politically connected firms.

In crony capitalist systems, businesses often engage in rent-seeking behavior, which increases profits through government intervention rather than through productive activities such as innovation or efficiency improvements. These interventions include seeking subsidies, tariffs, or other protectionist measures that benefit the business at the expense of consumers or competitors.

Crony capitalism distorts market competition by giving certain businesses an unfair advantage over others, creating barriers to entry for new competitors, stifling innovation, and reducing overall economic efficiency. Firms that are not politically connected may struggle to compete against those that receive preferential treatment from the government.

Crony capitalism often fosters corruption and nepotism within government institutions. Officials may prioritize the interests of their cronies over the public good, eroding public trust in government institutions and undermining the rule of law. Decisions are perceived as based on personal relationships rather than impartial criteria.

Ultimately, crony capitalism can lead to resource misallocation, slower economic growth, and worsened income inequality. Resources that could have been used for productive investment or public goods are instead diverted to politically connected firms, leading to their less efficient allocation and reduced welfare for society.

Crony capitalism is often criticized for undermining the principles of free-market competition, fairness, and transparency. It can diminish trust in government and business institutions and perpetuate a cycle of corruption and inequality. Efforts to combat crony capitalism typically involve strengthening transparency and accountability measures, reducing regulatory capture, and promoting fair market competition.

Crony capitalism corruption is a serious issue that has plagued many political systems, including the United States.

One common form of corruption in crony capitalism involves politicians accepting bribes, kickbacks, or other forms of illicit payments in exchange for favorable policies, contracts, or regulatory decisions that benefit certain businesses or individuals. This corruption threatens the integrity of the political process and lessens public trust in government institutions.

Politicians engaging in insider trading is a serious ethical and legal issue that also falls under the crony capitalism umbrella. Insider trading occurs when someone trades securities based on material, non-public information. When politicians use their access to privileged information for personal financial gain in the stock market, it raises concerns about fairness, transparency, and conflicts of interest.

While insider trading laws apply to everyone, including politicians, in some instances, lawmakers have been accused of using non-public information obtained through their official duties to make investment decisions. This could involve knowledge of upcoming legislation, regulatory actions, or other government policies that could significantly impact certain industries or companies.

> *"President Obama signed a bill preventing members of Congress from profiting from insider trading. Didn't you think that was already illegal?"*
> —Jay Leno

CHAPTER 14

What We Can Learn from Prominent Economists

In this chapter, to familiarize you with economic theory, allow me to introduce you to two prominent economists of our time. This will give you some basis of thought to apply to your own critical thinking.

Introducing . . .

FRIEDMAN

Milton Friedman (1912–2006), a prominent economist and Nobel laureate, was critical of crony capitalism—which we learned about in the previous chapter. He argued that genuine capitalism, characterized by free markets, competition, and limited government intervention, is essential for economic prosperity and individual freedom. However, Friedman believed that crony capitalism, which involves collusion between business and government to distort markets and secure special privileges, weakens the principles of capitalism and leads to inefficiency and corruption.[10]

Friedman was also a Nobel laureate and a highly influential figure in economics and public policy. Born in Brooklyn, New York, Friedman graduated from Rutgers University and earned his Ph.D. in economics from Columbia University. Throughout his career, he contributed significantly to economic theory, particularly in monetary economics, consumption analysis, and stabilization policy.[11]

Friedman's ideas often centered around the principles of classical liberalism and free-market economics. He was a staunch advocate for limited government intervention in the economy, believing that free markets allowed to operate without excessive regulation were the most efficient and equitable means of allocating resources and promoting economic growth.

Some of Friedman's most notable contributions to economic thought include monetary theory. Friedman's work on monetary economics, particularly his advocacy for a steady and predictable growth rate of the money supply, influenced central bank policies worldwide. He famously argued that fluctuations in the money supply were the primary cause of business cycles and inflation. Friedman developed the permanent income hypothesis, which suggests that individuals' consumption patterns are determined more by their long-term income expectations rather than short-term income fluctuations. This idea has had significant implications for understanding consumer behavior and designing economic policy.

_____

10   Friedman, Milton. Capitalism and freedom. with the assistance of Rose D. Friedman. Chicago: University of Chicago Press, 1964.

11   Soni, Aruni. "A Record High 58% of American Households Now Own Stocks." Business Insider. Accessed February 7, 2025. https://markets.businessinsider.com/news/stocks/record-high-american-households-own-stocks-investing-pandemic-markets-money-2023-10#:

He was a vocal advocate for free-market capitalism and individual freedom, writing extensively on the role of government in a free society and arguing for limited government intervention in economic and social affairs to preserve personal liberty and promote economic prosperity.

In 1976, Friedman was awarded the Nobel Memorial Prize in Economic Sciences for his achievements in monetary theory and his demonstration of stabilization policy's complexity.

Outside of academia, Friedman was known for his public advocacy and engagement in policy debates. He served as an advisor to two US presidents and was a frequent commentator on economic and political issues. His ideas continue to shape discussions on economic policy, specifically around monetary policy, taxation, and regulation.

Milton Friedman was one of the most influential economists of the 20th century and a staunch advocate for capitalism. He believed that, when properly implemented, capitalism was the most effective economic system for promoting individual freedom, prosperity, and innovation.

Friedman argued that capitalism fosters efficiency and innovation by incentivizing individuals and businesses to maximize profits. In a competitive market economy, businesses must continually innovate and improve their products and services to attract customers and remain profitable. This drive for efficiency and innovation can lead to economic growth and higher living standards for society.

Central to Friedman's advocacy for capitalism was its alignment with individual freedom.

He believed that capitalism empowers individuals to make their own choices and pursue their own interests without undue interference from the government or other central authorities. Friedman saw economic freedom as a fundamental component of personal liberty, allowing individuals to control their destinies and fulfill their potential.

Friedman advocated for limited government intervention in the economy, arguing that excessive government regulation and control stifles economic growth and innovation. He believed that the government should play a minimal role in the economy, primarily to enforce property rights, ensure the rule of law, and provide public services that the private sector cannot adequately supply. Some of these public services include the public school system, the National Airspace System (used to track aircraft), and the development of the National Aeronautics and Space Administration, known as NASA.

Friedman emphasized the importance of market mechanisms, such as supply and demand, in coordinating economic activity and allocating resources efficiently. He argued that competitive markets, guided by prices determined through voluntary exchanges between buyers and sellers, are the most effective means of coordinating the complex interactions of millions of individuals and businesses in the economy. Throughout his career, Friedman critiqued various forms of government intervention in the economy, including price controls, subsidies, and monopolies. He argued that such interventions often led to unintended consequences, distorted market signals, and reduced economic efficiency. Instead, he advocated for policies that promoted competition, free trade, and individual responsibility.

BASTIAT

Frédéric Bastiat was a prominent French economist, classical liberal theorist, and writer during the 19th century. He was born on June 30, 1801, in Bayonne, France, and died in Rome, Italy, on December 24, 1850. Bastiat is best known for advocating free trade, limited government intervention in the economy, and the concept of opportunity cost.[12]

One of Bastiat's most famous works is *The Law* (*La Loi*), published in 1850. In it, he argues that the law should protect individuals' rights and property rather than infringe upon them through redistribution or regulation. He believed that government intervention often skewed economic incentives and led to unintended consequences.

One of the unintended consequences Bastiat wrote about is minimum wage. He posited that while a policy to increase minimum wage may be intended to help low-wage workers, it could also lead to consequences such as businesses reducing their workforce or raising prices to offset higher labor costs.

Bastiat believed the supply side of the labor force would allow wages to rise as a market mechanism.

In this scenario, as the economy grows, the demand for goods and services will constantly need labor. As the requirement for labor increases, so, too, would the wages for the labor force.

Bastiat's writings were influential in shaping classical liberal thought and have continued to inspire economists and political thinkers around the world.

His emphasis on the importance of individual liberty and the dangers of protectionism and excessive government intervention remains relevant in contemporary debates on economics and politics.

---

12   "Frédéric Bastiat." Wikipedia, February 27, 2025. https://en.wikipedia.org/wiki/Fr%C3%A9d%C3%A9ric_Bastiat.

The "broken glass scenario" is often referenced in discussions about economic fallacies. Bastiat's essay, titled "What Is Seen and What Is Not Seen," was first published in 1850 and discusses the parable of the broken windows.

In "the broken glass scenario," a shopkeeper's window is broken by a careless child. The immediate reaction of onlookers might be to focus on the economic activity generated by repairing the window. Consider the glazier hired to fix the broken window, earning money for his services and that this visible economic activity might lead some to conclude that the broken window is beneficial for the economy, as it creates work and income for the glazier.

However, Bastiat's essay challenges this superficial analysis by highlighting *what is not seen*. While it's true that the glazier benefits from the repair work, the money used to pay him could have been spent on other goods and services if the window had not been broken. In other words, the shopkeeper would have had the opportunity to spend his money on something else, perhaps a new suit or a book, thereby supporting other businesses and stimulating economic activity in different sectors.

Furthermore, the shopkeeper's loss of wealth is reflected in the destruction of the window. He must now spend money to replace something previously intact without any additional benefit. The broken window diverts resources that could have been used for more productive purposes, ultimately leading to a net loss for society.

"The broken glass scenario" serves as a cautionary tale against focusing solely on the visible, immediate effects of economic events while ignoring the unseen consequences and opportunity costs. It underscores the importance of considering the broader implications of economic actions and policies, especially regarding their long-term impact on wealth creation and economic welfare.

Regardless of what allegory you get behind, all offer negative and positive consequences.

> *"Each of us has a natural right, from God, to defend his person,*
> *his liberty, and his property."*
> —Frédéric Bastiat

CHAPTER 15

Government Social Agenda

The shifts we experience in government policy hurt our overall economy. Many may argue that trying to bring balance from one side of the political spectrum to the other causes an uncertain economic impact in the short term.

Take, for example, the extraordinary steps the US government policymakers and the Executive Branch are taking toward the climate change agenda. The idea that the United States is abandoning the production of oil products may be an overgeneralization. While there is a growing recognition of the need to transition toward cleaner and more sustainable energy sources, such as renewable energy and electric vehicles, the US remains a significant producer of oil and oil products.

However, there are several reasons for a push to reduce reliance on oil production and consumption. Burning fossil fuels, including oil, is a major contributor to climate change and air pollution. As concerns about global warming and environmental degradation grow, pressure increases to shift toward cleaner energy sources to mitigate these impacts.

While the US still relies on imports to meet its energy needs, it aims to enhance energy security and reduce vulnerability to supply disruptions and price fluctuations in the global oil market by diversifying its energy sources and reducing its dependence on oil. Technological advancements in renewable energy, battery storage, and electric vehicles make these alternatives increasingly competitive with traditional fossil fuels. As renewable energy becomes more affordable and accessible, an economic incentive to invest in clean energy infrastructure grows.

Government policies and regulations play a significant role in shaping energy markets.

Initiatives to reduce greenhouse gas emissions, promote energy efficiency, and incentivize renewable energy development are driving the transition from oil to cleaner alternatives. Consumer preferences and market trends also influence the shift away from oil products. Increasing awareness of environmental issues and the desire for more sustainable lifestyles are driving the demand for electric vehicles, renewable energy, and energy-efficient technologies.

Is it feasible to abandon the production of oil products entirely? That's a great question many people are asking.

While it may not be realistic or practical to eliminate oil production in the near term, a growing recognition of the need to reduce reliance on fossil fuels and transition toward more sustainable energy sources can't be denied. This transition will likely be gradual and require concerted efforts from all global governments, industries, and individuals to overcome technological, economic, and political challenges. However, with the right policies, investments, and innovations, it is feasible to significantly reduce the use of oil products and accelerate the transition to a cleaner and more sustainable energy future. Oil Industry leaders are the best positioned to accomplish this goal.

Federal and local governments have significantly pushed toward solar energy and using solar panels and wind farms without considering adverse impacts.

And yes, there are adverse effects to alternatives. We have to get real about them to mitigate them and choose the best options for all.

CAN WE GO SOLELY SOLAR?

While solar panels are a popular and generally environmentally friendly source of renewable energy, they do have some adverse impacts worth considering.

Solar panel production requires raw materials such as silicon, silver, and rare earth elements. Mining and processing these materials can destroy habitats and pollute and deplete resources. Solar panel manufacturing is also energy-intensive. If the energy used in this process comes from fossil fuels, it can offset some environmental benefits.

The production of photovoltaic cells involves hazardous chemicals like cadmium, lead, and arsenic, among others. These are easily googleable facts, and urge you to spend a few minutes researching to learn more. If not handled properly, these substances can pose health risks to workers and contaminate the environment. Improper disposal of old or damaged solar panels can release toxic substances into the environment. Solar panel recycling processes are still developing and may not be fully efficient, which is another consideration when trying to figure out which energy sources should be prevalent.

Large-scale solar farms require significant amounts of land, which can disrupt local ecosystems and wildlife habitats, especially if they are built on previously undeveloped land. Solar energy production is also intermittent, depending on sunlight availability, and is naturally inconsistent due to weather conditions and seasonal changes. Effective energy solutions, like batteries, are needed to ensure a stable power supply. Manufacturing and disposing of batteries also has environmental impacts. In some cases, large solar farms contribute to the heat island effect, where areas become warmer than their surroundings due to heat absorption by the panels.

WHAT ABOUT WIND FARMS?

While a key part of renewable energy infrastructure, wind farms also have several adverse effects that should be taken into account. Wind turbines can pose a significant threat to birds and bats, which can be killed or injured by the turbine blades. Migratory paths can be affected.

The construction and operation of wind farms can disrupt local wildlife habitats, potentially changing local ecosystems and biodiversity. While wind farms have a low operational carbon footprint, the construction and maintenance phases do involve carbon emissions. Wind turbines have a lifespan of around 20-25 years. The decommissioning process generates waste, and the disposal of turbine blades, often made of non-recyclable materials, like fiberglass, which is non-biodegradable, presents environmental challenges.

Pile driving during wind turbine construction generates underwater noise that can harm fish and marine mammals, such as whales and dolphins, potentially leading to behavioral changes or physical injuries. When doing your research and developing your opinions, make sure to seek out credible sources. I have done my best to provide these to you throughout this book, in addition to backing up any assertions I make or encouraging you to google. I hope you develop this habit, as well.

THE SCIENCE OF THE EARTH

Skeptics of global warming argue that the Earth's climate has always undergone cycles of warming and cooling due to natural processes, such as volcanic activity, solar radiation variations, and ocean currents, which have affected significant climate changes long before industrialization.

Some point to periods like the Medieval Warm Period (roughly 900 to 1300 CE)[13], when temperatures were as warm or warmer than today, suggesting that current warming could be part of a natural cycle. Climate models are complex and make numerous assumptions about the future, including economic activity, energy usage, and technological development. Critics highlight past predictions, citing climate models that have not accurately forecasted future conditions and suggested a potential overestimation of future warming. Remember that those who provide data illustrating climate change may manipulate it to enforce their argument. One good rule of thumb to use to find out a corporation's or cause's agenda is to research who is funding a study. You may find a correlation to a group wanting to advance its agenda more than heal the Earth.

Some skeptics posit that variations in solar activity, including solar flares and sunspot cycles, are significant contributors to climate change. They argue that changes in solar radiation have a more direct and significant impact on global temperatures than human activities.

---

13   Author links open overlay panelDon J. Easterbrook, and Publisher SummaryRecent global warming (1978–1998) has pushed climate changes into the forefront of scientific inquiry with a great deal at stake for human populations. This chapter provides a geological evidence of recurring climate cycles and their impl. "Geologic Evidence of Recurring Climate Cycles and Their Implications for the Cause of Global Climate Changes-the Past Is the Key to the Future." Evidence-Based Climate Science, July 25, 2011. https://www.sciencedirect.com/science/article/abs/pii/B9780123859563100014.

> *Skeptics also argue that the economic costs of drastic measures to combat global warming may outweigh the potential benefits.*

They advocate for a more balanced approach that considers economic growth and energy needs.

Many argue that the number of volcanic eruptions above and below the surface are contributors to the climate change phenomenon, yet these events receive little media attention. Over the past five years, volcanic activity has been substantial, with a significant number of eruptions reported worldwide. According to the Smithsonian Institution's Global Volcanism Program, hundreds of eruptions occur each year. For instance, 2019 notes 75 volcanic eruptions recorded from 73 volcanoes[14] and 72 eruptions from 68 volcanoes in 2020.[15] Continuous degassing from volcanoes also contributes significantly to the global volcanic $CO2$ budget, although it pales in comparison to human activities.[16]

Supervolcanoes beneath the ocean are powerful geological features with the potential to cause widespread environmental and climatic impacts. Despite the challenges of studying these remote and deep-sea phenomena, advancements in technology and research are gradually improving our understanding of their behavior, risks, and the critical role they play in Earth's geodynamic and ecological systems.

---

14   "Global Volcanism Program: What Was Erupting in the Year...?" Smithsonian Institution | Global Volcanism Program. Accessed March 9, 2025. https://volcano.si.edu/faq/index.cfm?checkyear=2019&question=eruptionsbyyear.

15   "Global Volcanism Program: What Was Erupting in the Year...?" Smithsonian Institution | Global Volcanism Program. Accessed March 9, 2025. https://volcano.si.edu/faq/index.cfm?question=eruptionsbyyear&checkyear=2020.

16   "Volcanoes Can Affect Climate." USGS. Accessed March 8, 2025. https://www.usgs.gov/programs/VHP/volcanoes-can-affect-climate.

The Tamu Massif, one of the largest known volcanoes on Earth, is considered a large shield volcano (formed by successive lava flows). Deep in the Northwest Pacific Ocean, it has a footprint comparable to the state of New Mexico.[17]

In 2012, the Havre Seamount, part of the Kermadec Arc (a chain of active submarine volcanoes and small islands) near New Zealand, erupted in a massive underwater event, resulting in one of the largest deep-sea volcanic eruptions ever recorded. This event highlighted the explosive potential and hazards associated with submarine volcanic activity.[18]

Underwater volcanoes are linked to marine heat waves[19] and can increase the intensity of tropical cyclone activity.[20]

Volcanic eruptions can significantly alter marine habitats, affecting both the physical environment and biological communities. Hydrothermal vents associated with volcanic activity can support unique ecosystems, but eruptions can destroy these habitats. The release of sulfur dioxide and other volcanic gases into the atmosphere may form sulfate aerosols, which can reflect sunlight and cool the Earth's surface, potentially triggering short-term climate changes.

---

17   Post, The Washington. "Volcano the Size of New Mexico Found in Pacific Ocean." The Denver Post, April 29, 2016. https://www.denverpost.com/2013/09/06/volcano-the-size-of-new-mexico-found-in-pacific-ocean/.

18   The largest deep-ocean silicic volcanic eruption of the past century. Accessed March 8, 2025. https://www.science.org/doi/10.1126/sciadv.1701121.

19   Alexander, Ralph B. "Recent Marine Heat Waves Caused by Undersea Volcanic Eruptions, Not Human CO2." Science Under Attack, January 16, 2024. https://www.scienceunderattack.com/blog/2022/11/28/recent-marine-heat-waves-caused-by-undersea-volcanic-eruptions-not-human-co2-117.

20   The intensity of tropical cyclones may be impacted by large ... Accessed March 8, 2025. https://cpo.noaa.gov/the-intensity-of-tropical-cyclones-may-be-impacted-by-large-volcanic-eruptions.

All in all, the biggest questions concerning climate change study are simple and rational.

If climate changes are the direct cause of shifts in sea levels and are causing storm severity, resulting in tens of millions of dollars in damage to coastal areas, why is the development of these at-risk areas still allowed? Why can people and businesses still rebuild and develop after devasting storms wipe clean shores along the east and west coasts? Why does California not undertake a forest management system to reduce the risk of wildfires? Why have states allowed deforestation in many areas of the US to allow for the development of suburban areas?

These are questions we need answers to, and sadly, the only way we may make any headway in being more proactive and safe might come at the cost of more lives and dollars lost.

HOW WE COMPARE

France addressed its power needs with 56 nuclear reactors, which provide the country with a large portion of electricity.[21] Due to its successful nuclear program, France has an oversupply and is a net exporter of electricity. With the present technology, why hasn't the US addressed using nuclear facilities to enhance the power grid? Your guess is as good as mine.

Most recently, the Department of Energy's increased fossil fuel regulation has greatly weakened the US domestic production of fossil fuels. This is compromising US exports and forcing US allies to

---

21   "Nuclear Power in France." Wikipedia, February 22, 2025. https://en.wiki-pedia.org/wiki/Nuclear_power_in_France.

rely on countries with nefarious leaders for energy, which in turn is funding their war efforts. For example, Russia is selling natural gas to Germany while at the same time facing monetary sanctions imposed by the US for their aggression against Ukraine. Had the US continued to produce natural gas, Germany would not need to rely on the Russians for natural gas.

The argument is to move away from the use of fossil energy to a clean energy environment. In as much as these discussions may have valid points over the long term, the successful transition to a clean energy environment requires capital. It's critical to comprehend that the energy sector, not the government, is equipped to move the world to a cleaner energy grid.

These are rational questions that enhance the debate on environmental changes and how we address climate change. We need to continue talking about them and attempting to find the best answers if we are to see improvement.

"The best form of government is that which is most likely to prevent the greatest sum of evil."
—James Monroe

Our Unique United States

The United States' uniqueness can be attributed to its combination of free-market economy and social programs. The US is often called a melting pot because its people come from many different backgrounds and cultures, and there is such a wide variety of beliefs, values, and traditions. There is no such thing as the typical American – that's part of what makes it such an interesting place!

This blend reflects the American ethos of individualism, opportunity, and social responsibility.

The United States is known for its strong emphasis on free-market principles, where businesses operate with minimal government intervention, fostering competition, innovation, and economic dynamism. The country's history is replete with entrepreneurial success stories and industries propelled by market forces.

Despite its commitment to free markets, the US also maintains an extensive system of social programs aimed at providing a safety net for its citizens. These programs include Social Security, Medicare, Medicaid, and various welfare initiatives. While not as comprehensive as welfare offerings in some European countries, these programs demonstrate a commitment to addressing poverty, healthcare access, and social inequality.

The US is a global leader in private-sector innovation across various industries, including technology, healthcare, finance, and entertainment. The free-market environment encourages entrepreneurship and investment in research and development, leading to groundbreaking discoveries and advancements that benefit not only the country but the world at large.

The US labor market is characterized by flexibility and mobility, allowing workers to move relatively freely between jobs and industries. While this can lead to uncertainty for some individuals, it also fosters adaptability, innovation, and the efficient allocation of labor resources.

The American emphasis on individualism and self-reliance has shaped our free market and social programs. We hold a deeply ingrained belief of personal responsibility and the pursuit of success, as we recognize the importance of societal support for those facing hardship or disadvantage.

> *The balance between free-market principles and social programs in the US is often a subject of political debate and policymaking.*

Different administrations and political parties may prioritize these aspects differently, leading to shifts in government policies and programs over time.

PAYING HOMAGE TO SMALL BUSINESSES

Small businesses play a crucial role in the US economy, contributing significantly to economic growth, job creation, innovation, and community development. According to the US Small Business Administration (SBA), small businesses have generated around two-thirds of net new jobs in the country since the 1970s. They provide employment opportunities for millions of Americans across various sectors, including retail, services, manufacturing, technology, and healthcare.[22]

Small businesses contribute to economic growth by nurturing entrepreneurship, innovation, and competition. They introduce new products, services, and business models, driving productivity gains and stimulating consumer spending. By supporting local economies, small businesses also contribute to the diversification of industries and promote regional development.

Small businesses are hotbeds of innovation. With their agility, creativity, and flexibility, they often pioneer breakthrough technologies, processes, and ideas. Many of today's leading companies started as small startups in garages or dorm rooms. Innovation from small businesses fuels economic dynamism, drives industry evolution, and enhances competitiveness in the global marketplace.

Small businesses play a vital role in building vibrant communities. They contribute to the social fabric by creating opportunities for entrepreneurship, providing goods and services tailored to local needs, and supporting civic initiatives and charitable causes. Small businesses often forge strong ties with their communities, promoting social cohesion and enhancing quality of life.

The small business sector is diverse, encompassing a wide range of industries, ownership structures, and demographics. Small businesses owned by women, minorities, veterans, and individuals from other underrepresented groups diversity and encourage inclusion in the economy. Their resilience and adaptability help buffer the economy against shocks and downturns, as they can quickly adjust to changing market conditions.

---

22   "Homepage." Small Business Administration. Accessed March 8, 2025. https://www.sba.gov/.

Overall, small businesses are the backbone of the US economy, driving innovation, job creation, and economic prosperity. Supporting the growth and success of small businesses is essential for creating a thriving and resilient economy that benefits all Americans. Small businesses are also responsible for the bulk of tax revenues to local, state, and federal governments.

ECONOMIC PHASES

Over time, the US economy has experienced economic expansion and contraction phases, referred to as the business cycle, and epitomizing the natural fluctuation of economic activity. These cycles are characterized by periods of growth (expansion) and decline (contraction).

During an expansionary period, the economy is growing. Key indicators of economic expansion include increasing GDP (gross domestic product), rising employment levels, higher consumer spending, growing business investments, and overall consumer and business confidence.

GDP, a measure of economic growth, is usually measured by the velocity of new home sales, auto sales, inventories, and capital spending. As these activities increase over time, GDP rises, and the economy expands through a strong labor force, the effects trickling down to the consumer.

Several factors can contribute to this economic expansion, such as low interest rates set by the Federal Reserve, increased consumer and business confidence, technological advancements, government stimulus measures, and favorable global economic conditions.

Monetary policy is managed by a country's central bank, known as the Federal Reserve, and involves controlling the money supply, interest rates, and credit conditions.

Its effects on inflation are more direct and immediate. An example is quantitative easing, a process by which the Federal Reserve becomes a market participant and purchases US Treasury securities, using its purchasing power to maintain lower interest rates.

The Federal Reserve, often referred to as the Fed, is the central banking system of the United States. It was established by the Federal Reserve Act of 1913 and is responsible for conducting monetary policy, supervising and regulating banks, and maintaining the stability of the financial system.

The Federal Reserve System consists of several components of the board of governors. Located in Washington, D.C., the board comprises seven members appointed by the president and confirmed by the Senate. The chair and vice chair are among these members. Twelve regional Federal Reserve banks in major cities across the United States operate as decentralized branches of the Federal Reserve System.

Each US currency bill has special markings that tell you which Reserve Bank accounts for it. On $1 and $2 bills, the information is in the symbol to the left of the portrait. On all other bills ($5, $10, $20, $50, and $100), the Reserve Bank information is displayed in the letter-number code. This is done to account for the outstanding currency circulating throughout the globe.

As the US government funds its daily and monthly obligations, it issues Treasury notes and bonds to the public. Each bond carries a stated rate. Let's use this instance: a $1,000 Treasury bond sells at par, maintaining a $1,000 face amount at a rate of 3% for 1 year, with a payment of $30 per bond.

A fixed number of bonds are sold at auction, and in the wake of substantial demand, buyers bid on the price. If there is a strong demand for the bond, the price of the bond bid will increase, reaching a premium. While the price might change to $1,020 at a premium, the $30 payment would stay the same, but the yield would drop to 2.94%. If there is a soft demand and the auction does not attract investors, bonds can sell at a discount, pushing the bond price lower. A $1,000 bond might sell for $980 and keep the $30 payment, which would change the stated yield of 3% to 3.06%.

When the Federal Reserve decided to become an active market participant, it bought bonds daily, expanding its balance sheet to over $4 trillion in treasury securities. Some will argue the Federal Reserve, a quasi-government agency, has been funding government spending by keeping interest rates artificially low and becoming active market participants. This hasn't been done in years. The negative impact is excessive government spending and creating unsustainable national debt and deficits.

The Federal Open Market Committee (FOMC) sets monetary policy for the United States, including decisions on interest rates and open market operations. The Fed's primary responsibility is to conduct monetary policy to achieve stable prices, maximum employment, and moderate long-term interest rates. It influences the economy by adjusting the rate of federal funds, conducting open market operations, and setting bank reserve requirements.

The Fed supervises and regulates banks and other financial institutions to ensure their safety and soundness and to protect consumers. It establishes regulations related to capital requirements, lending practices, and consumer protection. It also oversees the nation's payment systems to ensure the smooth functioning of transactions and the stability of the financial system. The Fed monitors and addresses risks to financial stability, including systemic risks that could threaten the stability of the entire financial system.

The Federal Reserve operates independently from the federal government in its day-to-day operations, allowing it to make decisions based on economic data and analysis rather than political considerations. However, it is subject to oversight by Congress and is accountable for its actions. The Fed plays a crucial role in stabilizing the economy during economic downturns or crises. It can implement various monetary policy tools to stimulate economic activity, such as lowering interest rates, purchasing government securities, and providing liquidity to financial markets.

Governments and central banks use fiscal and monetary policies to manage economic conditions, including inflation.

Inflation is the rate at which the general price level of goods and services rises, decreasing the purchasing power of money. In simpler terms, the same amount of money over time buys fewer goods and services.

During an expansion, businesses often experience rising profits, leading to increased investment in equipment, hiring of workers, and greater production capacity. Rising consumer confidence typically results in increased spending on goods and services, further stimulating economic growth.

Contraction, on the other hand, is characterized by a decline in economic activity. Key indicators of an economic contraction include decreasing GDP, rising unemployment, declining consumer spending, reduced business investment, and lower consumer and business confidence.

These phases can occur due to various factors such as monetary policy tightening (increasing interest rates), external shocks like geopolitical tensions or natural disasters, decreased consumer spending due to uncertainty or a decline in disposable income, or a decrease in business investment due to pessimism about future economic conditions.

During a contraction, businesses may cut back on production, lay off workers, and reduce investment to mitigate losses. Consumers tend to spend less, leading to fewer demands for goods and services, further exacerbating the economic downturn.

> *It's important to note that economic expansions and contractions are natural parts of the business cycle and typically follow each other.*

Economists and policymakers closely monitor these fluctuations to implement appropriate monetary and fiscal policies to stabilize the economy and promote long-term growth.

Government intervention during economic expansions and contractions attempts to stabilize the economy and mitigate the negative effects of economic fluctuations. Unfortunately, partly due to political parties and their influence on how and where the government should act, this does not always happen.

Washington has been broken for decades, and its inability to work with respectful, rational discourse has been replaced by bitter partisan politics.

"Freedom is the open window through which pours the sunlight of the human spirit and human dignity."
—Herbert Hoover

The DEI Discussion

Another goal most academia and some policymakers aspire to is inducing fairness through identity politics.

I'm talking about DEI.

DEI initiatives, or Diversity, Equity, and Inclusion, are essential for fostering fairness, representation, and a sense of belonging in organizations and society. However, like any organizational strategy, it can have potential disadvantages or challenges.

Some individuals within an organization may resist DEI efforts, seeing them as unnecessary or threatening their status or privileges. There's a risk of tokenism, where organizations prioritize diversity for appearance rather than substance. Other individuals from underrepresented groups can feel used or undervalued. Focusing solely on metrics like diversity quotas may neglect the deeper cultural and systemic issues perpetuating inequality.

If DEI initiatives are poorly communicated or not understood by employees, they may not fully engage with or support them, undermining their effectiveness. In some cases, DEI efforts can trigger a backlash from certain groups that perceive companies as giving preferential treatment or an unfair advantage to specific demographics. Even with good intentions, DEI initiatives can fail if they're not implemented effectively or if there's insufficient commitment from leadership.

Focusing solely on one aspect of diversity (e.g., race or gender) can neglect individuals' intersecting identities and experiences, leading to incomplete solutions. Implementing DEI initiatives can require financial resources, time, and effort, which some organizations may perceive as burdensome, especially if they're facing other challenges. In organizations with deeply ingrained cultures or traditions, implementing DEI initiatives may face significant resistance from those accustomed to the status quo.

Despite challenges, DEI initiatives often have more benefits than disadvantages in promoting fairness, innovation, and organizational effectiveness.

Organizations need to approach DEI efforts thoughtfully and genuinely commit to creating inclusive environments for all. Today, we are seeing a reassessment of most forms of DEI in the private sector. One reason is the lack of talent. Although compassion is admirable, talent should be based on academic accomplishments and ability, regardless of color, orientation, or belief system. A business owner awarding a high-paying employment contract should not base their decision solely on identity.

The term "melting pot" has been used historically to describe the United States as a nation where people from diverse backgrounds come together, assimilate, and contribute to a unified American identity. However, over time, scholars and commentators have debated the accuracy and implications of this metaphor, and there has been a shift toward recognizing the United States as more of a "salad bowl" or "mosaic" of cultures, where diversity is celebrated, and maintaining different cultural identities alongside each other is more prevalent.

Today, I like to think that most people are striving for a greater acknowledgment of the richness and complexity of America's diverse cultural landscape. Rather than expecting people to assimilate into a singular mainstream culture, we can see a growing appreciation for various ethnic, racial, and cultural appreciation.

TRIBALISM

The concept of multiculturalism has gained prominence, emphasizing the coexistence of different cultural identities within society. Instead of melting into a homogeneous whole, individuals and communities are encouraged to maintain their distinct cultural traditions and identities. The disadvantage of this concept is that many people who look and feel the same will gravitate toward similar identity traits and settle into small enclaves or tribes.

Tribalism, in modern-day terms, refers to the strong loyalty and sense of identity individuals feel toward a particular group, often to the exclusion or detriment of others. This can manifest in various aspects of society, including politics, sports, religion, and social movements. People identify strongly with their "tribe" (e.g., political party, sports team, or cultural group) and often view those outside their tribe with suspicion or hostility. A strong "us vs. them" mentality, wherein group members are favored, and those in the out-group are viewed negatively, is evident.

Modern tribalism is often tied to identity politics, where political stances are closely linked to identities (e.g., race, gender, sexual orientation). Individuals may align with certain political or social groups based on these identities, leading to polarized communities. Society then becomes increasingly divided as different tribes hold strongly opposing views on key issues. Compromise and dialogue become difficult as each tribe views its position as morally superior.

Overall, modern tribalism reflects the human tendency to seek belonging and identity within a group, but it also highlights the challenges of fostering unity and understanding in an increasingly fragmented world.

A LOOK AT IMMIGRATION

Immigration patterns have changed, leading to a more diverse population and multiple cultural backgrounds. Rather than a predominantly European influx in the US as has been the case in previous centuries, contemporary immigration includes people from Asia, Latin America, Africa, and other regions, further enriching the cultural tapestry of the United States.

Over the past three years, the US immigration policy has been marked by significant shifts, controversies, and debates. The inauguration of President Joe Biden brought different expectations, changes, and reversals of significant immigration policies. Biden signed several executive orders aimed at reversing travel bans, fortifying DACA (Deferred Action for Childhood Arrivals), and halting construction of the border wall. He also initiated a review of other immigration policies. Some say this was done intentionally in a bold attempt to create havoc and that it led to debates over border security and immigration enforcement.

Proposed immigration reform legislation, including a pathway to citizenship for undocumented immigrants and measures to address root causes of migration from Central America, faced obstacles in Congress.

The unintended consequences, regardless of who is to blame, have led to an increase in human smuggling, drug trafficking, and unvetted South American gang migrants, terrorists, and criminals.

"Diversity: the art of thinking independently together."
—Malcolm Forbes

147

Globalization

The term "globalization" refers to the increasing interconnectedness and interdependence of countries, economies, cultures, and peoples around the world. Globalization is driven by advancements in technology, communication, transportation, and trade. Proponents of globalization argue that it nurtures economic growth, creates development opportunities, and facilitates cultural exchange and understanding.

Globalization has led to greater awareness and appreciation of diverse cultures around the world, influencing the US' attitudes toward diversity and contributing to the recognition of cultural pluralism.

Globalism supporters argue it is essential for addressing worldwide challenges such as climate change, pandemics, terrorism, and poverty, which transcend national boundaries and require collective action. Globalists believe that by working together on a planetary scale, countries can achieve greater prosperity, stability, and peace.

Critics of globalism, however, view it as a threat to national sovereignty, identity, and autonomy. They argue that globalist policies undermine democratic governance and transfer power from elected officials to unaccountable international bodies. Critics also express concerns about losing control over domestic policies, immigration, and economic decisions to supranational entities.

Government policies and initiatives have evolved to promote diversity and inclusion. Efforts to address systemic inequalities and promote equitable representation have also contributed to a more nuanced understanding of cultural diversity.

> *The idea of people coming to America and not assimilating into American culture has been a topic of debate, with arguments on both sides.*

While challenges are associated with a lack of assimilation, it's important to consider this issue's broader context and nuances.

THE ASSIMILATION DEBATE

A lack of assimilation can sometimes lead to social fragmentation or the formation of isolated ethnic enclaves within society. As discussed, this can hinder social cohesion and contribute to ethnic, cultural, or linguistic division. When individuals or communities do not assimilate into broader American culture, there may be a lack of shared values, experiences, and cultural references, making it more difficult to forge a common national identity. Assimilation into American society often involves acquiring language skills, cultural knowledge, and the social networks necessary for economic success. Those who do not assimilate may face barriers to employment, education, and social mobility, which can perpetuate economic inequality.

Assimilation can also impact political engagement and participation. When individuals feel disconnected from mainstream American society, they may be less likely to participate in civic life, vote in elections, or advocate for their interests through political channels.

Learning language is a significant aspect of assimilation, and individuals who do not learn English may face challenges in accessing education, employment, healthcare, and other essential services. Language barriers can exacerbate social isolation and limit opportunities for integration.

Lack of assimilation can sometimes lead to cultural conflicts or misunderstandings between different societal groups. Differences in values, norms, and practices may create tensions or barriers to social interaction and cooperation.

Non-assimilation can sometimes contribute to perceptions of immigrants or minority groups as outsiders or "foreigners," which may fuel prejudice, discrimination, or xenophobia within society.

It's essential to recognize that assimilation is a complex and multifaceted process that can vary widely depending on individual circumstances, cultural backgrounds, and societal factors.

Moreover, promoting assimilation should not entail erasing or devaluing cultural diversity.

Rather, efforts to facilitate integration should aim to create inclusive environments where individuals can maintain their cultural heritage while participating fully in the broader society. Ultimately, fostering social cohesion and inclusive citizenship requires balancing diversity and promoting shared values and experiences.

"Globalization is not a monolithic force but an evolving set of consequences—some good, some bad, and some unintended. It is the new reality."
—John B. Larson

Immigration

As of January 2020, the US has documented 11 million illegal migrants living here.[23] Handling such an influx of people into the US has been dynamic, with fluctuations influenced by factors such as policy changes, the pandemic, and court backlogs.

The issue of immigration remains multifaceted, and understanding the nuances behind these numbers is crucial if we are to have informed discussions and policymaking. The only question one can ask is *if America as a nation is inherently racist, with white supremacists and a history of xenophobia, why are people yearning to risk their lives only to be exposed to such hate?*

The founding principles of immigration in America are rooted in our nation's history, laws, and values. While these principles have evolved, several key ideas have consistently shaped America's approach to immigration.

"E pluribus unum," or Latin for "out of many, one," is a motto reflecting the idea that the United States is a nation of immigrants, built by people from diverse backgrounds who come together to form a unified whole.

America has long prided itself on being a nation that welcomes immigrants seeking freedom, opportunity, and a better life. The Statue of Liberty, with its famous inscription "Give me your tired,

---

23   Gilder, Lucy. "How Many Migrants Have Crossed the US Border Illegally?" BBC News, September 29, 2024. https://www.bbc.com/news/articles/c0jp4xqx2z3o.

your poor, your huddled masses yearning to breathe free," symbolizes this ideal.

While America welcomes immigrants, it also emphasizes the importance of following laws and regulations. Immigration laws establish criteria for who can enter the country, how they can do so legally, and their rights and responsibilities once they arrive.

Historically, immigrants have played a significant role in building America's economy. From the early settlers to waves of immigrants in the 19th and 20th centuries, newcomers have contributed their labor, skills, and entrepreneurship to help drive economic growth and innovation.

Immigration has enriched America's cultural landscape, bringing diverse traditions, languages, cuisines, and perspectives. Most see this diversity as a strength contributing to the nation's vitality and dynamism.

The principle of family reunification has been a cornerstone of US immigration policy. Many immigration laws prioritize keeping families together, allowing US citizens and lawful permanent residents to sponsor certain family members for immigration.

America has provided refuge to people fleeing persecution, violence, and war in their home countries. The principle of offering asylum to those in need reflects a commitment to humanitarian values and international obligations.

While these principles have guided US immigration policy, debates about immigration often center on how to balance competing interests, such as national security, economic concerns, and humanitarian considerations. As a result, immigration policy is subject to ongoing political and social discourse, with laws and regulations attempting to adapt to changing circumstances and priorities.

As our politics evolve and the undue influence of dark money affects political motivation, it's apparent how "crony capitalism" has bled into new areas of influence. Migration is a form of cheap labor, and lawmakers have even openly stated immigrants are needed to work in our restaurants, landscaping, and homes.

> *"Once I thought to write a history of the immigrants in America.*
> *Then I discovered that the immigrants were American history."*
> —Oscar Handlin

America's Homeless Crisis

Our federal budget allocates billions of dollars per year to support foreign aid to countries around the world while ignoring the homeless crisis here in America.

The American homeless crisis is a complex and multifaceted problem encompassing a wide range of factors, including economic inequality, housing affordability, mental health, substance abuse, and systemic failures in social services. One of the primary drivers of homelessness is the lack of affordable housing. Rising housing costs, stagnant wages, and insufficient affordable housing stock make it difficult for low-income individuals and families to secure stable housing. Gentrification and urban development also displace vulnerable populations and exacerbate homelessness in some communities.

A significant portion of homeless individuals struggle with mental illness, substance abuse disorders, or both. Limited access to mental health services, lack of affordable treatment options, and stigma surrounding mental illness contribute to this challenge.

Homelessness not only affects individuals on the street, but it has broader implications for communities. It strains public resources, including emergency shelters, healthcare systems, and law enforcement agencies. Homelessness can also contribute to public safety concerns, neighborhood blight, and economic disparities.

Efforts to resolve the homeless crisis in America require a comprehensive approach to address its root causes while providing immediate assistance and support to those in need. Investing in affordable housing initiatives, expanding access to mental health and substance abuse treatment, strengthening social safety nets, and implementing housing-first approaches that prioritize stable housing as a foundational answer to homelessness may be a multifaceted solution. Collaboration among government agencies, non-profits, community organizations, and private stakeholders is crucial to effectively address this complex issue.

The homeless crisis in California is particularly acute and has garnered significant attention due to the state's large transient population and visible encampments in urban areas. Mega donors and wealthy California residents have influenced policymakers with donations to prevent changes to residential building codes, preventing low-income housing units from being built—and theoretically, in some ways, emboldening what some argue are America's racist tendencies.

"Who are we as human beings if we ignore the suffering of others?"
—Dalai Lama

Is America Racist?

Let's revisit the question we were pondering earlier: *is America racist?*

Many will insist that America *is* a racist nation with deep-rooted privilege for those who ironically consciously rebuke racism. They argue the need for programs such as DEI to level the playing field. Academia and renowned university and college professors push the racist narrative without realizing the unintended consequences of further division within the nation.

The question of whether America is a racist country is complex and multilayered. Opinions vary widely depending on individual perspectives, experiences, and interpretations of historical and contemporary events.

The truth is that America has a long history of racism and racial discrimination, including slavery, segregation, and the systemic oppression of minority groups such as African Americans, Native Americans, Asian Americans, and Hispanic Americans.

While significant progress has been made in advancing civil rights and racial equality since the Civil Rights Movement of the 1950s and 1960s, the legacies of racism and inequality still shape social, economic, and political dynamics in the United States. Many scholars and activists argue that racism is deeply embedded in the structures and institutions of our society, leading to disparities and inequalities in areas such as education, employment, housing, healthcare, criminal justice, and wealth accumulation. Structural racism refers to how historical and systemic factors perpetuate unequal outcomes and opportunities for different racial and ethnic groups.

Racism can also manifest in individual attitudes, beliefs, and behaviors, including prejudice, discrimination, and bias against people of different races or ethnicities. While overt forms of racism may be less common today compared to the past, implicit bias and micro-aggressions still give rise to interpersonal and institutional discrimination.

Recent years have seen a resurgence of racial justice movements, such as Black Lives Matter (BLM), which have drawn attention to issues of police brutality, systemic racism, and racial inequality. These movements have sparked national conversations about race and racism and have led to calls for greater accountability, reform, and social change. Again, it's important to recognize that people's experiences of racism and racial discrimination can vary widely depending on race, ethnicity, gender, socioeconomic status, geographic location, and life experiences.

The BLM organization has also been under the microscope due to alleged corruption involving accusations of financial mismanagement, lack of transparency, or misuse of funds. Some allege corruption against its leadership within the movement.

In writing this book, I attempted to substantiate these claims, but that is all I could find: claims. There are rumblings of the misuse of hundreds of millions of dollars and a mansion purchased for BLM, but the recounting of these allegations is noted in right-leaning media. As I have remarked time and time again throughout this book, we must think critically. And we must research critically. This issue is no different. You can access the source I am providing at the footnote below,[24] but . . . and I'll say it once more . . . I encourage you to practice thinking (and researching) critically.

> *Another truth in America is that while some individuals may experience systemic racism and discrimination daily, others may be less directly affected or benefit from systems of privilege and advantage.*

Ultimately, whether America is considered a racist country is a subjective question that reflects ongoing debates about the nature of racism, the extent of progress toward racial equality, and the persistence of racial disparities and injustices. While America has made significant strides in addressing racism and advancing civil rights, many challenges remain in achieving true racial equity and justice for all.

In 2023, Black or African American individuals comprised about 14.4% of the total population of the United States.[25] This figure will fluctuate over time due to influences such as birth rates, immigration patterns, and changes in racial categorization. The non-white population of the United States, including individuals identifying as Black or African American, Asian, Hispanic, Latino, Native American, Pacific Islander, and those of mixed race, comprised a chunk of the total population that same year, with increasing percentages over time due to immigration, higher birth rates among minority groups, and changes in racial and ethnic demographics.

---

24   Southern, Keiran. "Black Lives Matter Mansion Is Symbol of Waste and Corruption, Say Critics." The Times & The Sunday Times, May 20, 2022. https://www.thetimes.com/article/black-lives-matter-mansion-is-symbol-of-waste-and-corruption-say-critics-5xw2cscz8.

25   Martinez, Gracie. "Facts about the U.S. Black Population." Pew Research Center, January 23, 2025. https://www.pewresearch.org/race-and-ethnicity/fact-sheet/facts-about-the-us-black-population/.

Hispanic or Latino individuals accounted for approximately 19.5% of the total population of the United States in this same year.[26] This demographic group includes individuals of Spanish-speaking origin or descent, regardless of race. The Hispanic population is one of the fastest-growing ethnic groups in the United States,[27] compounded by immigration, higher birth rates, and cultural factors.

"Not all of us can do great things.
But we can do small things with great love."
—Mother Theresa

---

26   Bureau, US Census. "New Estimates Highlight Differences in Growth between the U.S. Hispanic and Non-Hispanic Populations." Census.gov, June 28, 2024. https://www.census.gov/newsroom/press-releases/2024/population-estimates-characteristics.html.

27   "Latino Voices: Beyond the Numbers of America's Fastest-Growing Demographic." New America, October 22, 2024. https://www.newamerica.org/new-america/blog/latino-demographics-role-in-pluralistic-america/.

CHAPTER 16

Mainstream and Social Media Effects on Society

Mainstream media continues to unintentionally promote societal division today through its biased standard of news reporting. If you can believe it, at one time, the media reported the news. Today, it manufactures stories to create sensationalism and a "wow" factor. Editorial boards and news network executives promote biased content based on their personal affiliations and do so without conscious. We are learning the hard way that the unintended consequence of their self-awareness is eradicating critical thinking.

Self-awareness is the ability to perceive, understand, and reflect on one's thoughts, feelings, beliefs, motivations, and behaviors. It involves being conscious of oneself as a separate individual with a unique identity, including strengths, weaknesses, values, and goals. Self-awareness is looking inward and examining one's thoughts, emotions, and behaviors without bias or judgment while observing oneself objectively and recognizing patterns and tendencies. To be self-aware, you must understand your emotions and their triggers, intensity, and impact on your behavior. Self-awareness honors positive emotions like happiness and excitement and even negative emotions like anger and sadness. Beyond a more surface definition, self-awareness extends to understanding how one's actions, words, and behaviors affect others. It recognizes one's social dynamics, communication style, and interpersonal skills through a third-party observatory lens.

That's the good news.

But just as the dark intensifies the light, so does the light deepen the dark. Of course, there is a flip side: many use their self-awareness as a tool to motivate, manipulate, and indulge in exaggeration, leading to propaganda.

PROPAGANDA

Propaganda refers to the systematic and manipulative dissemination of biased, misleading information, ideas, or opinions. It is designed to influence a particular audience's attitudes, beliefs, and behaviors with an opposing belief. Governments, organizations, or individuals can use it to shape public perception, promote an agenda, or achieve specific goals.

Governments employing networks and social media utilize propaganda as a potent tool to manipulate public opinion, consolidate power, and advance their ideological agenda. Controlling information shared with the press, radio, film, and other forms of media ensures people will align with the ideology they seek (at least, those in charge hope it works that way). Many individuals who work within these organizations have personal relationships with the body directing the mouthpiece, which assists in coordinating messaging. Vilifying political opponents use entertainment forums such as late-night programming to promote agendas and attack political ideas in misalignment with the established bureaucratic system. In many instances, the educational system is levied to indoctrinate young people with an ideology rather than encouraging the expression of free-thinking ideas and conclusions.

As the government utilizes these outlets to promote its agenda, so, too, do outside foreign adversaries. These entities use our freedoms against us through organizations that promote misinformation dogma.

The question of whether mainstream media is propagandized or biased in its reporting is complex and nuanced. While media bias and influence are legitimate concerns, it's essential to approach news consumption with critical thinking skills, skepticism, and an awareness of the diverse array of media sources available. A well-informed citizenry relies on a free and independent press upholding journalistic integrity and serving the public interest—this is the way it used to be.

Mainstream media encompasses a gamut of news organizations, including newspapers, television networks, radio stations, and online news websites.

While some media outlets may have clear ideological or partisan leanings, few others strive to maintain journalistic integrity and objectivity in their reporting.

Not all media outlets are the same, and you can gain access to a variety of sources with different perspectives and editorial standards when you start to go down this rabbit hole.

Large corporations or conglomerates own many mainstream media outlets, which may influence editorial decisions and coverage priorities. Critics argue that corporate interests can shape media narratives and limit the diversity of viewpoints represented in the news. Additionally, advertisers and sponsors may exert influence over media content through financial incentives and pressure to conform to certain agendas.

Still, professional journalists are expected to adhere to ethical standards and the principles of accuracy, fairness, and impartiality in their reporting. Media organizations often have editorial policies and guidelines in place to ensure that news coverage is balanced, factually accurate, and free from undue influence. However, biases and subjective judgments can still influence the framing and presentation of news stories, leading to perceptions of partisanship among audiences.

Audiences may perceive media prejudice based on their ideological beliefs and preferences. Confirmation bias refers to the tendency to seek out information that confirms preexisting beliefs while disregarding or discounting contradictory evidence. In today's fragmented media landscape, individuals may gravitate toward media sources that align with their viewpoints, leading to the formation of ideological echo chambers (there's that word again!) and reinforcing partisan divides. In an era of misinformation and disinformation, fact-checking and media literacy are essential skills for evaluating the credibility and reliability of news sources. Fact-checking organizations and initiatives play a crucial role in holding media outlets accountable for accuracy and transparency in their reporting. Additionally, media literacy education can empower individuals to critically analyze news content, identify biases, and discern between credible journalism and misinformation.

"Don't believe everything you read on the internet just because there's a picture with a quote next to it."
—Abraham Lincoln

White House Staffers to Media Darlings

Several famous news journalists have worked under Democratic politicians or administrations, further muddying the waters of what non-bipartisan reporting means. Here are a few notable examples:

George Stephanopoulos: Stephanopoulos is a journalist and political commentator who served in multiple positions in the White House, most notably as the White House communications director for President Bill Clinton in the '90s. He later transitioned to a career in journalism and has worked as a correspondent and anchor for ABC News, including hosting *This Week with George Stephanopoulos*. [28]

Jay Carney: Carney is a journalist and former White House press secretary for President Barack Obama. Before joining the Obama administration, Carney worked as the Washington bureau chief for *Time Magazine* and as a senior political analyst for Time and CNN. [29]

Andrea Mitchell: Mitchell is a journalist and anchor who has covered politics for NBC News for several decades. While Mitchell is known for her extensive coverage of both Democratic and Republican administrations, she is married to Alan Greenspan, who served

---

28   "George Stephanopoulos." Wikipedia, March 4, 2025. https://en.wikipedia.org/wiki/George_Stephanopoulos.

29   "Jay Carney." Ballotpedia. Accessed March 8, 2025. https://ballotpedia.org/Jay_Carney.

as chairman of the Federal Reserve under Republican presidents. (I'd love to be a fly on the wall during their dinners.)[30]

Chris Matthews: Matthews was a journalist and television host known for his long-running show *Hardball with Chris Matthews* on MSNBC. Before his career in media, Matthews worked as a speechwriter for President Jimmy Carter and as a top aide to Speaker of the House Tip O'Neill.[31]

Jake Tapper: Tapper is a journalist and anchor who currently hosts *The Lead with Jake Tapper* on CNN. He has covered politics for various news outlets and worked as a White House correspondent during the Obama administration.[32]

> *These examples beg the question: How is it possible for a person who worked for a specific party for years with proven loyalty to now receive a paycheck from a news organization, where editors and program executives are also party loyalists yet are expected to report or program unbiased news?*

Isn't that the definition of conflict of interest?

Uri Berliner: Berliner, a journalist who worked at NPR (National Public Radio) before resigning in 2024, recently told *The Free Press* that the network "lost its way when it started telling listeners how to think." This, in the wake of NPR using its soapbox as a microphone to promote left-leaning liberal ideology, backed specifically by the Democratic Party.

---

30   "Andrea Mitchell." Wikipedia, March 6, 2025. https://en.wikipedia.org/wiki/Andrea_Mitchell.

31   Chris Matthews." Encyclopedia Britannica, February 21, 2025. https://www.britannica.com/biography/Chris-Matthews.

32   "Jake Tapper." Wikipedia, March 7, 2025. https://en.wikipedia.org/wiki/Jake_Tapper.

Berliner has been a senior business editor and contributed to NPR's business and economic news coverage, providing analysis and reporting on topics such as finance, technology, and industry trends. His work has been featured on NPR's flagship programs like *Morning Edition* and *All Things Considered*. Berliner's expertise in business journalism has made him a respected voice in the field, and his contributions have helped shape NPR's coverage of economic issues over the years.[33]

Several Republican aides have also transitioned from politics to careers in the media, offering insights and analysis from their insider perspectives. Here are a few notable examples of those who are walking a thin line just like their Democratic peers:

Nicole Wallace: Wallace served as the White House communications director under President George W. Bush and later transitioned to a career in media. She became a co-host of *The View* and a political commentator for MSNBC.[34]

Steve Schmidt: Schmidt was the senior campaign strategist and advisor to Senator John McCain's 2008 presidential campaign. He went on to become a political analyst for MSNBC and NBC News, where he often provides commentary from a conservative perspective critical of the Trump administration.[35]

Rick Santorum: Santorum became a political commentator for CNN after serving as Pennsylvania's Republican senator. He pro-

---

33   Berliner, Uri. "I've Been at NPR for 25 Years. Here's How We Lost America's Trust." The Free Press, April 9, 2024. https://www.thefp.com/p/npr-editor-how-npr-lost-americas-trust.

34   "Nicolle Wallace." Wikipedia, March 5, 2025. https://en.wikipedia.org/wiki/Nicolle_Wallace.

35   "Steve Schmidt." Wikipedia, February 22, 2025. https://en.wikipedia.org/wiki/Steve_Schmidt.

vided conservative viewpoints on various political issues before re-signing in 2021.[36]

Ana Navarro: Navarro, while not a former aide in the traditional sense, was a Republican strategist who now claims to be a centrist; her position seems to have moved left of center and no longer aligns with a conservative Republican stance. She's a frequent commentator on CNN and offer her center left perspectives on current issues.[37]

David Frum: Frum was a speechwriter for President George W. Bush and played a significant role in crafting the *Axis of Evil* speech (look it up). He later became a senior editor at *The Atlantic* and frequently commented on MSNBC, offering conservative insights and critiques.[38]

Joe Scarborough: Scarborough, a former Republican congressman from Florida, transitioned from conservatism to a more centrist or liberal-leaning ideology over the years. He and his wife, Mika Brzezinski, among others, co-host the MSNBC segment of news talk called *Morning Joe*.[39] While no single event caused Scarborough's shift in opinion, several factors likely contributed to his evolution in political ideology.

Scarborough served as a Republican congressman representing Florida's 1st congressional district from 1995 to 2001. During his time in Congress, he worked on conservative policy issues and aligned with the Republican Party. However, his experiences in Washington,

---

36 "Rick Santorum." Wikipedia, March 7, 2025. https://en.wikipedia.org/wiki/Rick_Santorum.

37 "Ana Navarro." The Institute of Politics at Harvard University. Accessed March 8, 2025. https://iop.harvard.edu/fellows/ana-navarro.

38 "David Frum." Wikipedia, February 27, 2025. https://en.wikipedia.org/wiki/David_Frum.

39 "Home." Joe Scarborough, October 10, 2023. https://joescarborough.com/.

D.C., and interactions with colleagues from both parties may have influenced his perspective on political issues.

After leaving Congress, Scarborough pursued a career in media. As a television host and political commentator, Scarborough has had the opportunity to engage with a plethora of perspectives and ideas, which may have led to introspection and a reevaluation of his own political beliefs.

The political landscape in the United States has evolved over the years, with shifting dynamics within the Republican Party and the broader political spectrum. Scarborough may have become disillusioned with the GOP's direction or disagreed with certain policy positions or tactics embraced by the party. Like many individuals, his personal values, beliefs, and life experiences may have influenced his political leanings.

As Scarborough navigated his career in media and public life, he may have reevaluated his positions on various issues and aligned himself with a different ideological perspective.

The other point to ponder is Scarborough's paycheck.

Scarborough is estimated to have a net worth of $25 million and an annual salary of $8 million.[40] Although an evolution in one's thought process is possible, we can't ignore that swinging from one extreme to another may have been spurred by monetary enticement. When an actor takes on a role as a serial killer in a movie, is the actor transformed into an actual serial killer? Or is he paid to perform? It's food for thought.

---

40 "'morning Joe' Hosts' Salaries: How Much Money Joe Scarborough, Mika Brzezinski and Willie Geist Make." Yahoo! Accessed March 8, 2025. https://www.yahoo.com/entertainment/morning-joe-hosts-salaries-much-092718278.html.

Despite his conservative start, Scarborough is now leaning more left-progressive, but I have suspicions about why he is supporting a drastically new platform. I can't think of any other reason why he would bash President Trump for four years, candidate Trump during his second run, and then visit Mar-a-Lago—except for the people telling him what to say to the public. And Trump offered to officiate Scarborough's wedding at the White House in November 2018 while still POTUS—so go figure that one out!

Overall, Scarborough's earlier disagreements as a Republican Congressman with then-Senator Biden likely stem from his earlier conservative principles and assessment of what he believed to once be in the country's best interest. Today's switch to praising Biden without offering criticism of any policy makes you wonder about a person's evolutionary journey . . . and then there's the nagging suspicion that there's more than what he's telling all of us.

Also, please note, these are *my* opinions of why Scarborough has changed his side of the fence. Please make sure to do your research to support your burgeoning opinions—and be open to your viewpoints changing as you learn more.

> *"So many reporters have blurred the line*
> *between reporting and editorializing."*
> —Andrew R. Wheeler

When Satire Meets Politics

Late-night comics hosting guests talking about current events and blending comedy with commentary on contemporary issues is a long-standing tradition in television. These shows often feature a mix of humor, satire, and serious discussions, making them a unique platform for addressing political and social topics.

Prominent figures from various fields—politicians, activists, journalists, and celebrities—often appear as guests. These interviews can range from light-hearted conversations to in-depth discussions on serious issues.

Late-night shows can influence public opinion and spark surprising conversations.

They reach a broad audience and often highlight issues that might not receive as much attention in traditional news outlets. Their timeliness allows them to respond quickly to breaking news and current events, offering real-time commentary that can be informative and cathartic for viewers. This immediacy makes the commentary feel relevant and urgent—although it might not be, and the hosts delivering the news may be underqualified and often biased.

Satire segments use humor, irony, exaggeration, or ridicule to criticize or highlight the absurdities and shortcomings of individuals, organizations, society, or political systems. They are often found in various media, including television shows, written articles, social media, and live performances.

EXAMPLES OF SEGMENTS:

<u>Stephen Colbert's "Opening Monologue"</u>: Known for his sharp political satire, Colbert often tackles major political events with wit and insight.[41]

<u>John Oliver's "Deep Dives"</u>: His detailed segments on *Last Week Tonight* covered topics like net neutrality and civil forfeiture, leading to increased public awareness and periodic policy change.[42]

<u>Trevor Noah's Interviews</u>: As the former host of *The Daily Show*, Noah's interviews with political figures and activists often delved into serious discussions about race, politics, and global issues.[43]

<u>Bill Maher</u>: Maher is a prominent figure in the realm of late-night television and political commentary. Known for his sharp wit and provocative style, he has built a career melding comedy with incisive political and social analysis. Maher's most notable platform is his show *Real Time With Bill Maher*, which has been on the air since 2003.[44] The show features a combination of monologues, panel discussions, interviews, and comedic segments. Maher's style is characterized by his willingness to tackle controversial topics and his no-holds-barred approach to political discourse.

Through *Real Time With Bill Maher* and his previous work on *Politically Incorrect*, Maher carved out a niche, combining humor with serious discussion to influence public discourse and offer a platform

---

41   "The Late Show with Stephen Colbert on CBS." CBS. Accessed March 8, 2025. https://www.cbs.com/shows/the-late-show-with-stephen-colbert/.

42   "Last Week Tonight with John Oliver: Official Website for the HBO Series." HBO. Accessed March 8, 2025. https://www.hbo.com/last-week-tonight-with-john-oliver.

43   Trevor Noah. Accessed March 8, 2025. https://www.trevornoah.com/.

44   "Bill Maher." Wikipedia, February 26, 2025. https://en.wikipedia.org/wiki/Bill_Maher.

for diverse viewpoints on current events. His approach to comedy and commentary continues to spark debate and engage audiences in meaningful conversations about the state of the world.

There is one most important aspect and assessment we can derive from late-night television. Although topics of discussion range across a broad scope of political and current events landscapes, most discussions are based on opinion and rarely fact-checked or verified. Debates can sometimes become heated, and often, the narrative is controlled. All present a left-leaning ideology.

Maher, a true self-proclaimed liberal, is the most honest. At times, he will call out the ideologies of guests who have aligned themselves with liberal ideas but have become irrational about their personal views. Maher respects and engages both sides of the discussion—and in this way, he advocates for his viewers, allowing them to make their own decisions and think critically about their ideologies.

YOUR WORLDVIEW, YOUR CHOICE

The program that appeals to you the most depends on your worldview. Remember, these aforementioned hosts are not experts on the topics they present. Guests, for the most part, are politicians or celebrities and lean on their political ideology. They live and reside in an echo chamber. Many times, facts are omitted, and truths are exaggerated to create greater division among the classes. But . . . you will, just as I will, want to watch a show that reflects your values and beliefs more than you won't. It's inherent in humans to gravitate toward what they can most closely identify with, and that's not a bad thing. It's just something to be aware of, so you can consciously expose yourself to varying viewpoints.

Many argue we are even predisposed to propaganda. If that's true, we must take the time to understand this impact. Propaganda takes various forms, including text, images, audio, video, and other media, and it is commonly used by governments, organizations, political groups, advertisers, and other entities to advance their interests.

It is fair to say most news-promoting television networks have evolved into echo chambers. Depending on the network, the host and guest are used to propagandize current events and sway public opinion. The common denominator is money. (Here's a hint as you are sharpening your critical-thinking skills: it's usually *always* about money.) Advertisers and influencers use platforms to their advantage, and whether intentional or not, they widen gaps between political disparities.

"People say satire is dead. It's not dead.
It's alive and living in the White House."
—Robin Williams

How the Nazis
Used the Media

The Nazis, under the German regime, extensively perverted the media into a tool for propaganda to shape public opinion, manipulate perceptions, and control information flow. They recognized the power of mass media, including newspapers, radio, film, and literature, to spread their ideology, reinforce their messages, and garner support for their policies.

Upon seizing power, the Nazis moved swiftly to control the press.

They shut down opposition newspapers, expelled Jewish journalists, and placed newspapers and publishing houses under their control or influence.

Joseph Goebbels, the minister of propaganda, played a crucial role in overseeing this process. Nazis recognized the power of radio as a mass communication tool and established the Reichs-Rundfunk-Gesellschaft (RRG), which centralized radio broadcasting under Nazi control. Radio broadcasts, including speeches by Hitler and Goebbels, were used to disseminate Nazi ideology, antisemitic propaganda, and news tailored to fit the regime's narrative.

The Nazi regime also utilized cinema as a powerful propaganda tool. Did you know that the Ministry of Public Enlightenment and Propaganda, directed by Goebbels, tightly controlled the film industry? He had his hooks into everything to brainwash the masses.

Propaganda films such as *Triumph of the Will*, directed by Leni Riefenstahl, glorified Nazi ideology and events like the Nuremberg rallies. Hitler even praised this film as an "incomparable glorification of the power and beauty of our Movement," likely thinking putting his name behind the work would drive loyalty to it. Another antisemitic film, *The Eternal Jew*, promoted racial hatred. Sadly, these weren't the only two films produced to promote this agenda.

The Nazi Party produced a vast array of printed materials, including posters, pamphlets, and books, to spread their propaganda messages far and wide. These materials often depicted racial stereotypes, glorified Nazi leadership, and demonized perceived enemies of the state, particularly Jews.

The regime also tightly enforced strict censorship laws. Any dissenting voices or information deemed contrary to Nazi interests were suppressed. Journalists and media professionals who did not toe the party line faced persecution or imprisonment.

The Nazis affected the arts and sought to influence cultural and artistic expression to align with their ideology. They promoted "Aryan" art while condemning "degenerate" art, which included works by Jewish and modernist artists. Writers, musicians, and other cultural figures were expected to produce content supporting the regime. Thankfully, attempts to harness the stunning diversity of creativity did not last. Today, we can appreciate art and artists from all around the world, and that appreciation requires no critical thinking.

It's another lesson: not everything needs to be overly examined. Some things are meant for pure enjoyment. In times of persecution, this is a quality and joy that can never be captured by another.

"The Nazis entered this war on the rather childish delusion that they were going to bomb everybody, and nobody was going to bomb them."
—Sir Arthur "Bomber" Harris,
British air officer of the "Saturation Bombing"

Forces at Work Today

I know I just rattled off a bunch of facts about horrific Nazis and that America today is reeling from a disruptive administration, but it is not a fair analogy to compare Nazi Germany to the present-day United States. Still, the fact that media outlets and social media platforms are taking bold steps in a poor attempt to camouflage their viewpoints and leanings is alarming and dangerous, primarily when fear is being used to create hysteria. In some instances, the downplaying of certain newsworthy stories is reported to protect the viability of a truth. Such truth may cause harm to a movement or, inversely, can be used to derail it.

The trend today in America is to control information as well as its sources for distribution. To better explain what I mean, let's hop in the wayback machine.

Gordon Gekko is a fictional character from the movie *Wall Street* (1987), portrayed by Michael Douglas. He is a ruthless and wealthy corporate raider known for his iconic line, "Greed is good." While he is not a real person, his character is often associated with the excesses and unethical practices of Wall Street in the 1980s.

Gekko's character could be interpreted as someone who values information as a tool for gaining an advantage in the financial world. In the movie, he famously says, "The most valuable commodity I know of is information." This statement reflects the mindset of someone who sees information not just as data but knows that it can be used to achieve power, influence, and wealth.

Gekko's character embodies the ethos of the "greed is good" mentality, where the pursuit of wealth and success justifies any means necessary, including manipulation and exploitation. In this worldview, information becomes a weapon to be wielded for personal gain, often at the expense of others.

Are the forces of complicit media gaining control of individuals' minds in America today? Are we still in that wayback bus? Have we not evolved beyond that point (fictional though it were)?

In the movie *Batman Forever*, the Riddler, whose real name is Edward Nygma, is depicted as a former employee of Wayne Enterprises who becomes obsessed with Bruce Wayne (Batman). In the movie, Nygma uses a device called the "Box" as a form of mind control. The Box is a high-tech device Nygma invented while working at Wayne Enterprises. It is capable of beaming television signals directly into the user's brain, effectively controlling their thoughts and actions.

> *Although the movie Batman Forever is a complete*
> *fabrication based on fiction, the use of mind manipulation*
> *begs a serious discussion.*

Today, social media and news outlets utilize various tactics that can be considered mind manipulation or persuasion techniques to influence public opinion, shape beliefs, and drive user engagement. They implore the use of complex algorithms to personalize users' feeds based on their preferences, behaviors, and interactions. By showing users content aligning with their beliefs and interests, platforms can create filter bubbles and echo chambers, reinforcing users' views and limiting exposure to diverse perspectives.

News outlets often use emotionally charged content to capture users' attention and evoke strong reactions, including sensationalist headlines, provocative images, and emotionally resonant stories designed to elicit fear, anger, or sympathy, thereby increasing engagement and virality. These algorithms tend to prioritize content that reinforces users' existing beliefs and preferences, leading to confirmation bias. Users are more likely to engage with and share content that aligns with their worldview, further entrenching their beliefs and potentially polarizing discourse.

News outlets may frame stories to emphasize certain aspects while downplaying or omitting others to influence how audiences perceive events. By controlling the narrative and framing issues in particular ways, media organizations can shape public opinion and agenda-setting.

They also employ persuasive design techniques, such as infinite scrolling, notifications, and autoplay features, to keep users engaged for longer periods and encourage habitual usage. These design choices can exploit psychological vulnerabilities and create addictive user experiences.

THE NEWISH PROPAGANDA PLATFORM

Social media platforms and news outlets can be used to intentionally spread false or misleading information—as has historically been the case when a bad actor takes the wheel. We've all seen fabricated news stories, conspiracy theories, and propaganda designed to deceive audiences and sow discord. These algorithms serving up such biased media, coupled with users' tendencies to seek out like-minded individuals, contribute to the formation of echo chambers. We now know this can exacerbate polarization and inhibit constructive dialogue.

> *Over the years, I have witnessed the slow deterioration of credibility, integrity, and honesty in news reporting, which has contributed to the continued division in society today.*

Now, social media practices peddle what sells and makes money, regardless of the subject—they are following right in the footsteps of our polarizing news networks.

And while corporate and social media technologies promote themselves as significant, you need to firmly believe that they are no more significant than you. You actually control them based on your interactions. Most of the information they spew out is not credible and is exaggerated—considered "noise." Why then, do we want to spend so much time ingesting it and, worse, believing it to be true—even when it means it may deteriorate our relationships?

You must understand that just because an event is reported, it does not constitute truth. Even if it is reported by other sources re-peatedly, it does not constitute truth. A popular saying goes, "A lie, if repeated enough times, can become believable, but in the end, it will still be a lie." As you think critically about what is presented to you, keep this saying in mind to help you stay impartial and open-minded to hear the facts.

Once the major news media outlets and social media platforms are influenced by one political party and used as a tool against po-litical opponents, deciding what is relevant, factual, and what news should be reported, they have threatened our democracy. I know it sounds like we should do something about that, doesn't it? Enter the argument of free speech, and the cycle continues.

My advice is to ignore the noise, live free, gather information, and do research. Do not allow yourself to be influenced by news personalities and political figures whose only goal is to manipulate you into becoming one of their followers.

Politicians will constantly use terms such as "saving our democ-racy" or "defending democracy." While on the surface, that sounds promising and hopeful, beware of anyone inducing fear as a tactic to support their personal agenda.

Our founding fathers created a system that so far, has lasted 249 years. The greatest threat to our existence stems from unintended consequences created by US foreign policy to inflict American policy on other countries and societies.

In 2001, following the attacks of 9/11, the US Administration at the time, in a bold attempt to bring the culprits to justice for the murder of thousands of people and billions of dollars in damages, decided to launch an attack on Afghanistan, the hotbed of terrorism in the world.

Rather than making the primary focus destroying the ability to carry out further attacks, the administration convinced legislators to expand the operations to the sovereign country of Iraq.

After years of costly wars, death, and destruction, thousands of displaced refugees, and the unsettling of the Middle East, the US and the world are no safer today than before the 9/11 attacks. Some believe the US is now more of a target than it has been at any other time in history. On the flip side, many good ideas exist and continue to be brought forth to help lead us away from that end—and they have all been created with good intentions. It is smart to focus on what we have in front of us to help make us better, don't you think?

From education to technological advancements to politics to climate change, globalization, and societal changes, the media has created echo chambers to distract viewers and listeners from the importance of self-preservation. The unintended consequences can lead to complete societal disruption, division, and noise intensity, wreaking havoc on individual freedoms and loss of rights.

Much of the "noise" is intended to distract individuals, leading to more division among the masses, communication deteriorating, leadership disappearing, and insignificant people manipulating the hordes into backing causes that do not promote the good of all society.

The desire to succeed requires focus and the insight to avoid distraction, which can reduce your ability to network, seek out opportunities, and create relationships with individuals who may share different beliefs. Learn to shut off the garbage. You cannot create wealth or success if you are at the mercy of trashy content.

Everyone is different, and approving or disapproving of their beliefs is not up for debate. Although some topics should be avoided and not tolerated in extreme cases, the agreement to respectfully disagree (for the most part) can be achieved.

"The media is the most powerful entity on earth. They have the power to make the innocent guilty and make the guilty innocent, and that's power. Because they control the minds of the masses."
—Malcolm X

CHAPTER 17

Dollars and Sense
The Failing Educational
System in the US

You may be of the age where you are getting ready for college or are there already. Maybe you are working in the trades or researching the best steps to take to secure a job in a specific field. It doesn't matter your role in society or what you are currently doing; education affects us all—even when we are not the students. So, I urge you to read this chapter to determine if we are doing our young people a disservice as they embark on a new life stage or if you feel they are genuinely properly prepared to start the next phase of their academic journey. Think about how you feel about what you are about to learn—the true reality of our education system. And don't forget to regard this new information critically.

ARE KIDS REALLY READY FOR COLLEGE?

Social and emotional preparedness for college varies greatly among high school graduates and depends on numerous factors, including individual experiences, upbringing, education quality, and personal development. While some may feel well-prepared for college's social and emotional aspects, others may face challenges transitioning to a new environment.

High school provides a social environment where students interact daily with peers and teachers. However, college often presents a different social dynamic, with larger class sizes, more diverse student populations, and increased independence. Some high school graduates may find navigating new social relationships and settings challenging, while others may adapt more easily. Regardless, students need to be socially and emotionally mature to navigate changes.

Students must also be prepared to navigate one of the largest financial obligations of their lives—especially if they have not earned a scholarship, grant, or other endowment to reduce or eliminate student debt.

To understand why school debt is out of control and students are being squeezed into lifelong crippling financial burdens, we need to understand how the educational system works, what is valued, and who and what benefits from these staggering loans.

Let's start by better understanding how our nation views education and what it's spending on programs and initiatives.

JUST THE FACTS

Understanding the cost of the US educational system and its bureaucracy created over the years will give you insight into why it is not working. In short, dollars are spent with no common sense, resulting in the unintended consequences of a failing system.

The United States Department of Education (ED) was created on October 17, 1979, when President Jimmy Carter signed the Department of Education Organization Act into law. The department officially began operating on May 4, 1980. The ED was established to strengthen the federal commitment to ensuring access to equal educational opportunity for every individual and to improve the co-ordination and management of federal education programs.[45] This is a worthy cause.

Google a breakdown of the US Department of Education's federal budget for fiscal year 2024, and you'll see it amounted to approximately $79 billion in discretionary funding—an increase of 13.6% from fiscal year 2023.

In addition to this budget, every state in the United States has its own Department of Education and budget allocation.

Google also tells us that the average cost per student in K-12 public schools in the United States for the 2022-2023 school year was approximately $ 15,633 per student.

The US Department of Education plays a central role in shaping the nation's education system and ensuring that all students have access to high-quality educational opportunities that prepare them for success in school, work, and life. It has an estimated 4,400 federal employees[46] and is known for having the smallest staff of the cabinet agencies and an annual budget of $268 billion[47].

45   "United States Department of Education." Wikipedia, March 8, 2025. https://en.wikipedia.org/wiki/United_States_Department_of_Education.

46   "About the U.S. Department of Education." aaec. Accessed March 10, 2025. https://aaec.ed.gov/about-the-us-department-of-education#:~:text=ED%20was%20created%20in%201980,well%20as%20monitoring%20those%20funds.

47   "What Does the Department of Education Do?" USAFacts. Accessed March 10, 2025. https://usafacts.org/explainers/what-does-the-us-government-do/agency/us-department-of-education/.

The average school in the United States spends $20,387 per pupil, the third-highest amount per student (after adjusting for local currency values) among the 37 other developed nations in the Organization for Economic Co-operation and Development (OECD).[48]

According to Global Citizens Solutions, the United States ranks 12th in educational quality.[49]

In summary, the United States is one of the highest spenders per capita on education yet students are graduating from high school and college with disappointing results.

The federal branch of the US Department of Education plays a significant role in shaping and overseeing federal education policy and programs nationwide. The Department of Education is responsible for developing and implementing federal education policies and initiatives to improve educational outcomes for students at all levels, from early childhood through postsecondary education. This includes initiatives related to curriculum standards, assessment, teacher quality, school accountability, and student financial aid.

ED administers a wide range of grant programs providing funding to states, school districts, institutions of higher education, and other organizations to support various education-related activities and initiatives. These grant programs address priorities such as improving academic achievement, closing achievement gaps, supporting students with disabilities, and promoting innovation in education.

---

48   Hanson, Melanie, and Fact Checked. "U.S. Public Education Spending Statistics [2025]: Per Pupil + Total." Education Data Initiative, February 8, 2025. https://educationdata.org/public-education-spending-statistics.

49   Garrido, Manuel. "The 15 Countries with the Best Education: 2025 Ranking." Global Citizen Solutions, March 4, 2025. https://www.globalcitizensolutions.com/countries-with-best-education/.

ED is responsible for enforcing federal civil rights laws prohibiting discrimination based on race, color, national origin, sex, disability, and age in education programs and activities receiving federal financial assistance. This includes investigating complaints of discrimination, conducting compliance reviews, and providing technical assistance and guidance to schools and colleges.

The department collects and disseminates data on various aspects of education, including student enrollment, demographics, academic achievement, graduation rates, and postsecondary outcomes. This data is used to inform education policy and practice, conduct research, and monitor the progress of educational goals and objectives.

ED administers federal student financial aid programs that provide grants, loans, and work-study opportunities to help students and families pay for postsecondary education. Programs such as the Pell Grant, Direct Loan Program, and Federal Work-Study Program provide billions of dollars in aid to millions of students annually.

The Department of Education develops regulations and guidelines to implement federal education laws and ensure compliance with statutory requirements. It also provides technical assistance and guidance to states, school districts, and higher education institutions to help them understand and comply with federal education laws and regulations.

The government has played a significant role in expanding access to higher education through federal student loan programs. While these programs were initially intended to help students from low-income families afford college, they have also enabled colleges and universities to increase tuition fees without facing significant consequences. As a result, the availability of easy-to-access federal loans has contributed to the rising cost of tuition, and colleges have little incentive to control costs since students can borrow more to pay for education.

The student debt crisis in the United States is a complex issue with multiple contributing factors, and the role of government policies is one aspect of the problem.

Here's how government actions have played a role in exacerbating this crisis:

For-profit colleges and universities have been a major contributor, compounding this situation. They often charge high tuition fees for programs that may not provide quality education or lead to meaningful employment opportunities. Despite concerns about predatory practices and low graduation rates at some for-profit colleges, government oversight and industry regulation are limited, allowing these institutions to continue to enroll students who often end up with high levels of debt and few job prospects.

Unlike other forms of debt, such as that accrued through credit cards or mortgages, student loans are not typically dischargeable through bankruptcy. Lack of bankruptcy protections means that borrowers facing financial hardship often cannot discharge their student loan debt, leading to long-term financial burdens and increasing the likelihood of default. While this policy was intended to protect taxpayers from losses on defaulted loans, it has contributed to this predicament by trapping borrowers in a cycle of debt.

In recent decades, state funding for public higher education has declined significantly in many states. As a result, public colleges and universities have increasingly relied on tuition revenue to fund their operations, leading to tuition increases that have outpaced inflation. While this trend is not solely attributable to government actions, it has contributed to the overall rise in college costs and student debt burdens.

The federal student aid system is complex and difficult for students and families to navigate. So, some students may borrow more than they need or take out high-interest private loans when more affordable options are available.

Additionally, applying for financial aid and managing student loans can be burdensome, confusing, and frustrating for borrowers.

While government policies have helped many students access higher education, they have also encouraged the student debt crisis by enabling tuition increases, failing to regulate predatory practices, and creating barriers to debt relief for struggling borrowers. Addressing the student debt crisis requires a multifaceted approach, including reforms to federal student loan programs, increased oversight of for-profit colleges, and efforts to make higher education more affordable and accessible for all students.

Now for the facts on the roles institutions are playing . . .

University endowments can vary greatly and are influenced by investment performance, donations, and spending policies. As of January 2022, the total endowment assets for US colleges and universities numbered in the hundreds of billions of dollars.[50]

College and university endowments can be funded by various sources, such as:

<u>Alumni and Donors</u>: Many endowments receive contributions from alumni, philanthropists, corporations, and other donors who want to support the institution.

---

50   Moody, Josh. "College Endowments Dropped in Fiscal Year 2022." Inside Higher Ed | Higher Education News, Events and Jobs. Accessed March 8, 2025. https://www.insidehighered.com/news/2023/02/17/college-endow-ments-dropped-fiscal-year-2022.

<u>Foundations</u>: Some university endowments are funded by private foundations supporting educational institutions and initiatives.

<u>Government Grants and Contracts</u>: Universities may receive grants and contracts from government agencies for research and other purposes, which can contribute to their endowment funds.

<u>Investment Returns</u>: Endowment funds are often invested in various financial instruments such as stocks, bonds, and real estate. The returns generated from these investments can grow the endowment over time.

<u>Tuition and Fees</u>: A portion of student tuition and fees may go toward funding university endowments, although this is typically a smaller allotment than other sources.

<u>Royalties and Licensing</u>: Universities may earn royalties and licensing fees from their faculty members' and researchers' intellectual properties, which contribute to endowment funds.

University endowments are typically funded through a combination of donations, investment returns, and other sources of revenue, like donations and groups such as the Tides (seeded by mega Democratic donor George Soros), the Bill and Melinda Gates Foundation, the Rockefeller Brothers Fund, and the Libra Foundation (founded by Nick and Susan Pritzker).

These groups show a direct correlation between the policies a university adopts and the funds it receives, not earmarked to offset tuition costs but to promote faculties with left-leaning ideologies. Colleges and universities catalyze student activism by nurturing critical thinking, fostering empathy, providing resources, and creating spaces for dialogue and action on pressing social issues. Alumni who have been involved in activism during their college years can serve as mentors and role models for current students, providing guidance, networking opportunities, and inspiration.

Colleges have historically been hotbeds for activism, with students holding protests, demonstrations, and debates on campus. Freedom of speech and expression are typically protected on college campuses, allowing students to voice their opinions and challenge authority.

Colleges may offer courses, workshops, and seminars explicitly focused on activism, social justice, and community organizing. Additionally, events like conferences, panels, and guest lectures feature activists who use this platform as a form of manipulation. Colleges actively support student activism by providing resources, funding, and logistical aid for events, campaigns, and initiatives aimed at social change.

The argument can be made that through social engineering, colleges and universities manipulate young, impressionable minds to fight for the causes professors, alumni, and donors believe in. Are donors motivated to fund causes rather than support educational institutions? What do you think?

THE BUSINESS OF COLLEGE SPORTS

The NCAA (National Collegiate Athletic Association) is a non-profit organization that regulates student-athletes and athletic programs at colleges and universities in the United States and Canada. It governs various sports, from basketball and football to tennis and swimming, and sets rules and guidelines for eligibility, recruiting, scholarships, and competition formats. It also organizes and oversees numerous national championships across different divisions, such as Division I (the highest level), Division II, and Division III. The NCAA plays a significant role in shaping the landscape of collegiate sports in North America.

The NCAA generates revenue from various sources, including media rights deals, sponsorship agreements, ticket sales, and licensing fees. While I don't have exact figures for the NCAA's total revenue in 2023, I can estimate it based on available data and trends.

Let me explain.

In recent years, the NCAA's largest revenue source has been its media rights deals, particularly for the NCAA Men's Basketball Tournament, commonly known as March Madness. These deals involve broadcasting rights with major television networks such as CBS and Turner Sports.[51] In 2016, the NCAA signed an extension with CBS and Turner Sports worth approximately $8.8 billion over 14 years, indicating the significant value of these media rights.[52]

Additionally, the NCAA generates revenue from sponsorships and partnerships with companies seeking to associate their brands with collegiate athletics. These sponsorship agreements can encompass a broad spectrum of categories, including apparel, financial services, and consumer goods.

While revenue from ticket sales and other sources also contribute to the NCAA's overall income, media rights deals and sponsorship agreements are typically the largest revenue drivers.

Given these factors, I would estimate that the NCAA's total revenue in 2023 was likely in the range of several billion dollars. How-

51   "Finances." NCAA.org. Accessed March 8, 2025. https://www.ncaa.org/sports/2021/5/4/finances.

52   Lewis, Jon. "CBS, Turner, Extend NCAA Deal through '32; No Changes to Final Four." Sports Media Watch, January 5, 2021. https://www.sportsmediawatch.com/2016/04/cbs-turner-ncaa-march-madness-eight-year-extension-final-four-cable-2032.

ever, without access to specific financial reports or data for that year, this estimate remains speculative. For the most accurate information, it would be necessary to consult the NCAA's financial statements or industry analyses of collegiate athletics' finances.

How college athletes get paid has changed rapidly, especially in the United States. Traditionally, college athletes weren't allowed to receive compensation beyond scholarships, which covered tuition, room and board, and other expenses. However, there have been significant shifts in this paradigm.

One notable change came through the NCAA adjusting its rules to allow college athletes to profit from their name, image, and likeness (NIL). This means athletes can now earn money from endorsement deals, sponsorships, appearances, and other opportunities based on their personal brand. These changes opened avenues for athletes to capitalize on their fame while still in college.

Subsequently, legal and legislative changes at the state level in the US have occurred. Several states have passed laws allowing college athletes to profit from their NIL rights, although the NCAA has not yet implemented its own nationwide rules. These state laws vary in specifics but generally allow athletes to pursue endorsement deals and other opportunities without risking their eligibility.

Discussions and debates intend to determine whether college athletes should be considered employees of their universities and thus be entitled to more traditional forms of compensation, such as salaries. This debate touches on issues of fair compensation, the amateurism model in college sports, and the significant revenues generated by college athletics programs.

Changes in NCAA rules, state laws, and ongoing debates about fair compensation have evolved how college athletes are getting paid. These developments have opened new opportunities for athletes to monetize their talents while navigating complex legal and regulatory frameworks.

Some students receive scholarships to participate in athletic competitions. While athletic scholarships can provide valuable opportunities for student athletes to pursue higher education while competing in sports, they are typically awarded to a relatively small percentage of high school athletes, particularly at the Division I and II levels. The availability of athletic scholarships can also vary by sport. High-profile sports like football and basketball tend to offer more scholarships compared to sports with smaller budgets or lower levels of competition. The NFL and NBA do not have minor league programs. Colleges and universities investing significantly in these two sports know they are engaging in sports entertainment to generate revenues.

HOW DO WE SOLVE THE STUDENT DEBT CRISIS?

In contrast to the US, Europe's higher education system is diverse and varies from country to country, although it shares some features and structures across many European nations.[53] Research-focused institutions offer a wide menu of undergraduate, graduate, and doctoral programs in various fields of study, specializing in science, technology, engineering, and mathematics (STEM).[54] These institutions may focus on practical or vocational education, offering programs more directly applicable to the workforce.

---

53   "School Systems in the European Union." La Fondation Robert Schuman le centre de recherches et d'études sur l'Europe. Accessed March 10, 2025. https://www.robert-schuman.eu/en/european-issues/212-school-systems-in-the-european-union.

54   "Relevant and High-Quality Higher Education." European Education Area. Accessed March 10, 2025. https://education.ec.europa.eu/education-levels/higher-education/relevant-and-high-quality-higher-education.

Tuition fees vary widely across Europe. Higher education is largely publicly funded in some countries, such as Germany and Norway,[55] and tuition fees for domestic and EU students are either very low or non-existent. Many European countries have established quality assurance agencies or systems to ensure that higher education institutions maintain high standards of teaching, research, and administration.[56] Institutions may undergo periodic evaluations or accreditation processes to assess their quality and adherence to national or international standards. Many European countries invest in research through government funding agencies, grants, and partnerships with private sector organizations.[57]

As you may conclude, European colleges and universities offer a much better solution to its citizens than the United States—unless you are an athlete.

In my opinion, forgiving student debt will not solve the student debt crisis in America and will send a terrible message to taxpayers. The government could hold US colleges and universities to a higher standard through the Legislative Branch. It could investigate the fact that some schools have profited from money laundered through vulnerable students looking for a better opportunity.

The government could also lower student loan interest rates and allow students to enroll in a payback program when they serve in

55   Funding higher education: A view across ... Accessed March 10, 2025. https://www.eurashe.eu/wp-content/uploads/2022/02/modern-funding-higher-education-a-view-accros-europe.pdf.

56   "ESG • Enqa." ENQA, October 2, 2024. https://www.enqa.eu/esg-standards-and-guidelines-for-quality-assurance-in-the-european-higher-education-area/.

57   "Innovation, a European Asset to Be Valued." Zabala Innovation, December 20, 2023. https://www.zabala.eu/news/innovation-european-asset-to-be-valued/.

one of the military branches after attending college or a university. Finally, a mandate could allow students to attend a two-year college program through community colleges, where elective courses are much more affordable.

Education is an important aspect of one's life. The demand for quality education has caused the unintended consequence of driving up the costs of learning to unaffordable levels. The good news is that with the introduction of technology, fewer people need a 4-year college degree to achieve financial success. Many individuals have found careers in employment that do not require the cost or time of college to become productive in society. Vocational institutions offer education for trades in demand, and pay salaries higher than those of individuals graduating with 4-year college degrees.

High school guidance counselors promote college education to students as one-size-fits-all. Unfortunately, more students are finding after accumulating debt and graduating with irrelevant degrees, that employment is unavailable, time has passed, and a redo is not an option. All of this leaves the student in a terrible financial circumstance.

When it comes to your education, design a plan that fits your financial ability, and take advantage of the system. Do not allow the system to take advantage of you.

"Pay off your debt first. Freedom from debt is worth more than any amount you can earn."
—Mark Cuban

CHAPTER 18

The Final Word

As I have stated multiple times within these pages, my goal in writing this book is to empower and inspire you to take the necessary steps to change your life.

Let's do a recap.

Affecting change in your life can be a powerful and transformative process. Clearly define what aspect of your life you wish to change. It could be related to career, health, relationships, personal growth, or any other areas. Start with small, manageable actions. Gradual progress can lead to lasting change and prevent you from feeling overwhelmed. Regularly assess your progress and adjust as needed. Celebrate small victories along the way, and be open to adapting your plan if circumstances change. Flexibility allows you to navigate obstacles more effectively; don't be afraid to pivot if you sense a redirect is needed. Recognize that setbacks and challenges are a natural part of the process. Learn from them as opportunities to grow. Imagine yourself achieving your goals. Visualization can help reinforce your commitment and motivation.

Empower yourself with self-motivation—the inner drive or personal initiative needed to achieve goals and act without the need for external encouragement or pressure. Self-motivation will push you to pursue your aspirations and overcome challenges, even when faced with difficulties or a lack of immediate rewards.

Belief in your abilities plays a significant role in self-motivation. People with high self-efficacy and a positive mental attitude have confidence in their skills and capabilities. Make this a part of your internal makeup.

Understanding the concepts described to you in this book on managing money will assist you in creating wealth.

- Remember to budget your income.
- Keep your wants and desires to a minimum.
- Focus on your needs.
- Stay away from unnecessary expenses and purchases such as gambling, new expensive cars, elaborate designer clothing, and accessories.
- Networking with others outside your family and building personal relationships opens opportunities for growth.
- Realize life has distractions, especially those present in social media.
- Focus on real-life events which have a direct impact on your life.

Creating wealth is a long-term strategy and requires time, patience, and discipline.

A very good friend once asked, sarcastically, if my financial philosophy was built on the premise of *buy, hold, and hope*. Unfortunately, many individuals investigating a different philosophy expect to search for a quick fix while trying to avoid risk; this is not always possible. Any investment brings risk, but there are ways to mitigate it. Try not to confuse mitigating risk with risk avoidance. They are not the same. Effective risk management can help prevent or lessen the negative impact of unexpected situations. Many successful S&P 500 companies have created wealth for numerous investors over time. These investors believed in long-term companies' fundamentals and were well rewarded.

Finally, investing requires continually monitoring your plan, risk, and potential impact. Regularly reviewing and updating risk assessment ensures new risks are identified, and existing ones are managed effectively. Research, at times, can add value, but sources can be exaggerated and make unfounded claims. Always be wary of get-rich schemes and focus on successful strategies. Use your critical thinking skills, resist immediate gratification, and commit to riding out your financial investments. When you combine investment acumen with the knowledge gained from this book, you will be on your way to building positive habits to influence more wealth in your life.

I wish you years of abundance and success.

"Never regret a day in your life. Good days bring you happiness, and bad days bring you experience."
—Unknown

WHAT TO CONSIDER WHEN HIRING A FINANCIAL PLANNER
(FROM A FINANCIAL PLANNER)

Successful investing requires an understanding of risk, patience, and a rational, decisive process. Not everyone is proficient in grasping the complexities of investing—which is completely understandable as the rules and regulations, not to mention the recommendations and best practices, can get pretty granular and specific. This doesn't mean you shouldn't spend time learning about investing or trying out the waters of investing (no matter your age) and creating wealth. Working with a professional may have its benefits, but there is no comparison to undertaking your own complete due diligence process.

After researching, many individuals believe they are capable of investing on their own. But before you go off and start loading up your investing shopping cart, I advise that you seek out a professional to guide you and answer the questions you will undoubtedly have.

Without professional training, it can be challenging to make informed decisions, leading to potential losses. Researching investments and managing a portfolio can take a significant amount of time and effort. Individual investors might be more prone to making emotional decisions, such as panic selling during market downturns. Professional investors have access to advanced tools, research, and networks that individual investors typically do not.

Without diversification and proper risk management strategies, you can take on more risk than necessary. And without the insights and timely information professionals possess, you might miss out on lucrative opportunities.

BANKS

Many banks, brokerage firms, and insurance companies offer financial planning services. Consider consulting with a financial advisor or planner to help you develop an investment strategy tailored to your goals and circumstances.

Until 1999, you could not invest through your bank, but many now offer these services. In 1999, Congress repealed the Glass-Steagall Act that prohibited banks from offering investment and insurance services to retail consumers. The Glass-Steagall Act was originally passed in 1933 after the Great Depression when many people lost all their savings and investments when banks went bankrupt.[58]

And while many banks offer investing services, they have been added to their original offerings and often have a steeper price tag—after all this is not their bread and butter.

---

58   Heakal, Reem. "Glass-Steagall Act of 1933: Definition, Effects, and Repeal." Investopedia. Accessed March 8, 2025. https://www.investopedia.com/articles/03/071603.asp.

In today's world of compliance, many banks are exempt from regulations others must adhere to, such as whether the advisor working for the bank is a "fiduciary." This is an area where you need to beware. The five-second explanation is that a fiduciary, by definition, is a person who has your best interests at heart. But people differ in their opinions of what this means. What's good for one customer—an upsell of insurance services to save them time from researching this area—might not be good for another and could be viewed as predatory. What do you want fiduciary to mean to you? Whatever it is, do your research to make sure whoever you pick to start learning how to invest is in it to help you succeed.

If you work with a bank advisor, understand that uncertainty about their conflicts of interest must always be considered. How can you be sure that your advisor is offering you the best advice and not just the advice that benefits the bank—or the advice that the bank has made mandatory? Does your advisor have free will to present different products to you that are to your best advantage?

INSURANCE AGENTS

An insurance agent is the intermediary between a general or life insurance company and the client. They sell insurance policies depending on customers' financial needs and life milestones. The agent should have a vast knowledge of insurance policies and expertise in suitable plans that complement clients' financial goals. Most products sold through insurance agents or brokers are commission-driven.

The main disadvantage of commission-based brokers is that the incentive to sell a product is not rooted in the best interests of the client (there's that fiduciary debate again). There is no motivation for the broker to remain engaged with the investor. Whereas a fee-based arrangement keeps the advisor engaged in the process over the long haul.

Working with a professionally licensed individual requires due diligence. Some questions you can ask are:

- *Are your fees commission-based or advisory?*
- *Are you a fiduciary?*
- *What licenses do you possess, and do you have any designations?*
- *Can you describe for me the relationship we will have moving forward?*
- *Do you have an engagement contract?*

Further due diligence can be achieved by searching the Financial Industry Regulatory Authority known as FINRA. Searching the licensed individual's name will reveal a complete work history and their license disclosures.

Deciding whether to invest on your own or use a financial planner depends on several factors, including your financial knowledge, time availability, investment goals, and comfort with managing your finances.

Some pros of investing on your own are avoiding fees associated with financial planners. You can also have complete control over your investment decisions, which opens the opportunity to learn and grow your financial knowledge as you tailor investments to your exact preferences.

It might sound simple, but research and management of investments can be time-intensive and require a good understanding of financial markets and investment strategies. If you choose to go it alone with your investments, there is a significant chance you'll make impulsive or emotionally driven decisions. Many people panic when they see their hard-earned money take a nosedive, and, of course, the instinct is to protect what you've earned, but there is wisdom in riding it out, in averaging rates of return. As you mature, it gets easier to sit still and watch—I promise!

Besides being too impulsive, many people lack the expertise to optimize their investment strategy or plan for complex financial situations.

If you are confident in your financial knowledge, have the time to manage your investments, and prefer control over your financial decisions versus a guide giving you advice, you can achieve financial independence.

If you need professional guidance, have a complex financial situation, or prefer to delegate financial management to an expert, choose someone you can have a strong business relationship with.

"A man who does not plan long ahead
will find trouble right at his door."
—Confucius

ACKNOWLEDGMENTS

When I decided to write this book, I shared my concept with my colleague Nora Gillis. She and I have two very different views on society. We share the same insight with respect to investing and our admiration for successful individuals, and we have tremendous mutual respect for one another, both professionally and personally, but we differ in other areas—although we make it work!

It was Nora who recommended I work with Hilary Jastram, my editor. During my journey with Hilary, we developed such a great working relationship, I still, to this day, do not know her societal or political leanings, yet we worked closely for months on this project, motivated and excited to achieve this final book project.

We can all have our differences in life, but for us to co-exist in a healthy society, we must always be open to an honest, open dialogue and respect for one another regardless of our leanings.

I hope I have imparted that this is possible through this book, and I thank you, dear reader, for taking the time to read it.

ABOUT THE AUTHOR

Mario Sicari is a stalwart in the realm of investments. With over 30 years of unwavering dedication and expertise, he has honed his craft as an investment professional, navigating the complexities of financial markets with seasoned insight and precision.

Mario's wealth of experience encompasses various market cycles, economic climates, and investment landscapes, affording him a unique perspective few can match. Throughout his illustrious career, he has weathered storms and seized opportunities, demonstrating a remarkable ability to adapt, innovate, and thrive in the face of change.

As you inspire yourself from his journey and glean insights from his wealth of knowledge, he is confident you will uncover invaluable lessons and timeless principles to transcend generations in the ever-evolving world of investing.

Mario has been a leader in establishing a successful wealth management firm. He has also engaged audiences as a public speaker, empowering individuals with the art of investing and self-motivation.

Early in his career, Mario worked as the vice president of business development for a well-established broker-dealer. He had the vision and a dedicated team to build a successful asset management firm.

Years later, he turned his attention to building a wealth management firm. Today, his team manages over $300 million in private client accounts.

His views on geopolitical and market risks have made his firm one of the premier advisories in independent wealth management channels. Mario's firm has been named one of the top wealth management firms in New Jersey for many years, and he continues to lay down the foundation to reach this accolade for many more years to come.

DISCLOSURE

The views and opinions expressed in the content of this book are solely those of the author, Mario Sicari. Statements can be proven to be true or false using objective evidence. Facts are universal and true in all cases and for all people. All examples of mutual funds and stocks are not intended as a solicitation. These examples are intended to be used in an educational format. The author and publisher make no attempt to recommend, buy, sell, or purchase. Should anyone consider the purchase of any mutual fund, stock or any other security, they should consult with a licensed individual and tax advisor.

Mario Sicari is a registered representative with Cetera Financial Specialist. He is a chartered life underwriter, chartered financial consultant, accredited investment fiduciary, and a charter leadership fellow. He is a certified instructor with NASBA (National Association of Board Accountancy), offering continuing education credits to accountants and certified public accountants. He is a certified life, health, property casualty, and annuity instructor in the State of New Jersey, offering continuing education to licensed brokers in the State of New Jersey. He is also a licensed mortgage representative in the State of New Jersey NMLS# 269690. FINRA CRD# 2365508.

1.) Securities offered through Cetera Financial Specialists LLC (doing insurance business in CA as CFGFS Insurance Agency LLC, CA insurance license #0E28878), member FINRA/SIPC. Advisory services offered through Cetera Investment Advisers LLC. Cetera firms are under separate ownership from any other named entity. 201 WEST PASSAIC STREET, SUITE 301, ROCHELLE PARK, NJ 07662.

2.) The views stated in this book are not necessarily the opinion of Cetera Financial Specialists LLC or Cetera Investment Advisers LLC and should not be construed directly or indirectly as an offer to buy or sell any securities mentioned herein. Due to volatility within the markets mentioned, opinions are subject to change with notice. Information is based on sources believed to be reliable; however, their accuracy or completeness cannot be guaranteed. Past performance does not guarantee future results.

3.) Neither Cetera Financial Specialist LLC nor any of its affiliates offer tax or legal services.

www.ingramcontent.com/pod-product-compliance
Lightning Source LLC
Chambersburg PA
CBHW071557210326
41597CB00019B/3292